The Lady and the Dragon

The Lady and the Dragon

A Historical Update of
End-Time Prophecies

Loren Henry Wilson

Copyright © 2011 by Loren Henry Wilson.

Library of Congress Control Number: 2011901121
ISBN: Hardcover   978-1-4568-5779-0
             Softcover   978-1-4568-5778-3
             Ebook   978-1-4568-5780-6

All rights reserved. No part of this book may be reproduced or transmitted in any form or by any means, electronic or mechanical, including photocopying, recording, or by any information storage and retrieval system, without permission in writing from the copyright owner.

This book was printed in the United States of America.

To order additional copies of this book, contact:
Xlibris Corporation
1-888-795-4274
www.Xlibris.com
Orders@Xlibris.com

Contents

Preface		7
Chapter 1:	The Watchers	9
Chapter 2:	At the Time of the End . . .	14
Chapter 3:	In the Days of These Kings . . .	23
Chapter 4:	Power Groups at the End of Time	29
Chapter 5:	The Four Horsemen of Revelation	45
Chapter 6:	Testing the Seals	56
Chapter 7:	Issues at Stake and an Action Preview	67
Chapter 8:	The Pause that Protects	75
Chapter 9:	The Trumpets of Change	83
Chapter 10:	The Second Trumpet	91
Chapter 11:	The Third and Fourth Trumpets	98
Chapter 12:	The Fifth Trumpet	105
Chapter 13:	The Sixth Trumpet	115
Chapter 14:	The Three Woes and the Seventh Trumpet	122
Chapter 15:	The Two Witnesses	129
Chapter 16:	The Lady and the Dragon	138
Chapter 17:	The Beast	148
Chapter 18:	Evangelism and Reformation	154
Chapter 19:	One Hour with the Beast	163

PREFACE

This book is about the fulfillment of Bible prophecy and the end of the world (or the end of this present age, we should say). Or we could say that it is a history of the church written before it even started. What it *is not about* is stars falling to the earth, seas turning to blood, and everybody getting one last chance to get saved (although that is indeed popular stuff to read about these days). But such predictions about future catastrophes do not tell us much about *where we are now located in God's timetable of world events* as time winds down to the end.

So we will instead be dealing with prophecies about events that have already happened or are presently happening before us in our very own time—and are well recorded in our history books and newspapers. As the Lord taught us in Isaiah chapter 41, our seeing the actual fulfillment of the Bible's prophecies right before our very own eyes, or even in recent history, is one of the most important ways that God has given us to be awed and impressed with him, his works, and his ways. It is a faith-building experience, and that is something the church desperately needs today. To apply most of the Book of Revelation, for example, to the future as is often done, does not answer this need nor provide this blessing. What it does do is rob Christians of needed confidence in the god who says that things will happen and then provides the fulfillment of them in ways that can be accurately recorded and believed. The Lord Jesus said, "I have told you before it is come to pass, that when it is come to pass you might believe."

Some of these chapters have been lifted out of two books that have been published by Waymarks Radio Ministries and, for several years, have been distributed by mail to people living around the world who have found us on radio and Internet. One book is an interpretive study guide through the Book of Revelation and the other one through parts of Daniel. I have taken certain topics from these two works that not only seem to flow together well, but also will give some meaningful highlights of how wars and political arrangements have, for the last two thousand years, fit like a glove upon what the ancient prophets wrote about so long ago.

The first chapter is a teaser about angels and the end-time that is written from a sort of secular viewpoint. Hopefully, it will stir the appetites of you, the readers, to continue on to investigate the rest of the story.

Loren Henry Wilson
Waymarks Radio Ministries International www.waymarks.org

Chapter 1

The Watchers

A True Story, Not Science Fiction

At this very moment, while you are reading these lines, our world is being watched. It is under the constant and unrelenting surveillance of unearthly beings who are from outer space and who come from a world that is far distant from our own.

This is not a new thing. These beings have, in fact, been at the work of monitoring our planet for all human history, and they have even intervened in global affairs on many occasions. We have an abundance of preserved records that prove it to be so. And their purpose is clear. They are even now planning the process for an eventual, forceful takeover of our planet Earth. And the time for it is not far-off. Who are they? They are called by many names. One of them is *the Watchers*.

HOW CAN WE KNOW?

How do we know this is true? The evidence for it all is written in a book, one that was dictated from outer space to human writers who lived a very long time ago in ancient times. This book has been amazingly preserved for thousands of years, and when carefully studied and deciphered, it tells a revealing story about the interest that the Watchers have in us and in our planet.

As strange as this may sound, there have always been people living on Earth who knew about the existence of the Watchers. Actually, their presence has been revealed and their story told many times, but most of the world has not believed it. The time has now come for their existence and their announced agenda to be told plainly so that all the people of the world can prepare themselves for what is about to happen. *Time is getting very short.*

All of us need to know the facts about the Watchers. Most of the time, they are invisible to the eyes of humans, but the preserved record tells us much about them. These invisible beings are not all alike nor do they all follow the same plan and purpose. They all inhabit either the light side or the dark side of our universe, and they are all committed to pursuing global and universal concepts that are actually opposite in nature. For this reason, there have been many battles fought between them.

THE WATCHERS' AGENDA

The common agenda of the Watchers, both present and final, is to participate in the control and government of all the inhabitants of the universe through the operation of the standards that they understand to be true and valid. One side seeks to operate by artificial, unreal truth by which they design to gratify only themselves and their like fellowship. If they were to achieve domination, they would bring all things that exist to an end of absolute disorder and material randomness, like a decaying corpse that was once a living beautiful animal. They think this is truth.

The Watchers who inhabit the light side, however, are seekers and champions of absolute truth, and their agenda is for true order to remain and for new manifestations of true order to constantly occur so that existence is filled with meaning instead of disorder. The struggle between these two sides is very real and shows up on the pages of history. *However, only one side will win. Only one can.*

THE ULTIMATE POWER

But there is more. As wise and as powerful as the Watchers are, there is an ultimate Power that is above them. This Power has determined what the course for the future will be and which of these two great forces will be in final, total control of our world, our galaxy, and all things that exist.

This huge Power is ultimate, perfect, and expressive and has purposed and appointed the determined end that all life forms that exist in the universe will finally flow into a comprehensive whole that is full of meaning, order, beauty, and truth. Those of the Watchers who are on the light side of the universe understand this, and they are wholly giving themselves to the accomplishment of it.

What kind of identity is this great Force that is at the top of our universe? Is it a mindless, random power, or is it an actual Being of force and intelligence? For all of man's history, the inventors of philosophies and religions have grappled with this question. And the answer to it has always been available. It is found in the same book that contains the information about the Watchers—the ancient, preserved book that contains the answer to this question for those who care enough about finding it.

It shows that there is indeed a creative and designing Being who exists totally of and in himself and who is responsible for all things that exist. It is he who controls the Watchers and who manages the course of events, both large and small. Even though he also is invisible to our human eyes, he has, on occasion, visited the earth, and he has announced that he will be coming back with the Watchers when the time arrives for the final planned takeover. What is he called? Those people who hate him use his name as a curse word. But he has many names. They all describe him for who he is and what he does. One of them is *I am*, and that is because he exists outside the confinement of time and space.

IMPLANTED SEEDS

At the dawn of human history, this creative Being began to implant seeds of himself into the bodies of human beings. Gradually, in every generation, the seeds would begin to grow and to dominate the thoughts and actions of the people in whom they were implanted. As a result, these people became different from other people who exist only in the earthly norm.

Throughout earth's history, the ones with the seeds have exhibited the nature of the Ultimate Being, whereas the rest of humanity has exhibited the nature and program of the Watchers on the dark side of the universe. This disparity between the peoples of the world has perpetually been the cause of wars and social upheavals, and it continues to be so even to this day as these unseen forces continually guide the events that we call history.

THE SPECIAL SEED

Many centuries ago, the *I am* implanted a single very special seed of himself into a human woman. The Son that was born from this union had no earthly father, and he had qualities that far surpass those of any other human being who has ever lived, before or since. The *I am* officially designated this special Son of his to be the future Ruler of this world, as well as the heir of all creation.

Centuries ago, because of the jealousy of some of the rulers of this world—who are aligned with the dark side of the universe—this special Son was rejected and brutally killed. However, the One who is *I am* intervened, raised his Son back to life and drew him up and out of this world into the unseen sphere of the universe where he and the Watchers have their habitation. He is still there today, waiting for the appointed time when he and the *I am* will return, along with a huge force of the Watchers, when they will forcefully take control of this whole world, putting down all authority and power.

Amazingly, at that same time, all those people of the world who have the seed of the *I am* implanted within them will rise in the sky to meet them as they descend. Those who are dead will be brought back to life, and those who are alive will join them, all in the sky, meeting the *I am*, his Son, and all the Watchers who are of the light side.

Immediately, the governments of all the nations of the earth will be put down, and the special Son of the Great *I am* will be crowned as the Ruler of all this world. He will reign over the earth for a thousand long years, along with all those who are the seed of the *I am*, and there will be a time of peace, prosperity, and scientific advancement such as the people of the world have never imagined. After that, there will be other great events that will occur, and a new age will begin that defies human thought to describe.

BUT IS IT ALL TRUE?

Is all this true? Yes, it is. And it is all there in the book your fathers and mothers used to read—*the Bible*. The Watchers, of course, are angels (Daniel 4:13), good and bad angels, the bad ones called demons or devils. The *I am* is God himself (Exodus 3:14), and the special seed is his Son Jesus Christ. The people with the implanted seeds are the children of God of all parts of the world and ages of time. They are implanted by being spiritually born of God (John 3:3). All others are "children of the devil" as Jesus referred to them in John 8:44. The struggle for supremacy is real, and the end is now closer than it has even been. How close is it?

Bible prophecy tells us much about this, as the following chapters will show.

Were you able to figure out the symbolic imagery in the foregoing chapter? Perhaps we needed to interpret some of the details for you although much of it would be plain to an active and functioning Christian reader of the Bible—but not, of course, to everyone.

CHAPTER 2
At the Time of the End...

Is there really a God in heaven? Does he actually rule his creation and reveal himself to mankind? And would he ever discuss his existence with us mortals, who are the mere creatures of his designing work? The answer to those questions is yes, and if we were better readers of our Bibles and especially the prophets of old, we would have more of the answers about God that we need for our security and direction in these unbelieving times.

The prophet Isaiah took up this cause about acquiring the knowledge of God in chapter 41 of his book, putting forth an argument from God himself about how man can better know about his existence and his awesome works. In that passage, he compared himself to the gods of old time to which the ancient people often went with their heavy questions about life. And he ridiculed their ignorant behavior, just as he ridicules many of us today and the god of humanism that we are pursuing and worshipping. We can hear him laughing if we listen carefully.

GOD PROVES HIMSELF

This useful tool that God extends to us in Isaiah 41 is the actual dated fulfillment of the prophecies about future times that he has given to us. With this tool, we can see him at work across centuries of time and be absolutely certain that the whole world is indeed in his hand and going in his direction. And he casts sarcasm at the gods of our own making who cannot see, hear, speak, or tell us anything about what the future holds. He said, "Show us things that are to come, that we may know that you are gods..."

The recorded fulfillment of prophecy is not just for the old times. Today, we can see how events of the generation of those people now living were recorded in the dark writings of the prophets in the Bible. It takes a little effort and careful prayer, but these things can be seen.

The prophet Daniel lived and wrote his prophecies in the fifth century before Christ. He had an insatiable desire to know what God was going to do with Israel and with the world. Some world-class prophesied events had already started happening by that time, and Daniel saw the destruction of the last of the nation of Israel at the hands of the Babylonians. Then during his own lifetime the (known) world empire of Babylon swiftly declined and fell to the rising tide of Persian domination. It was an era that was filled with constant international upheavals as new empires arose and swept across the known world. Jeremiah called it the time of God's controversy with the nations (Jeremiah 25:31).

God, in his wisdom and purpose, gave the prophet Daniel several mighty visions that took in some very long spans of time. The last of these long prophecies in Daniel's writings is also the most lengthy and comprehensive one. It fills all of chapters 11 and 12 in the Book of Daniel. God dispatched a special messenger to tell his servant, "What will befall your people in the latter days: for yet the vision is for any days" (10:14).

THE LATTER DAYS

This prophecy began with events that were contemporary to Daniel's own time. From that point, the flow of words went on to reveal the fall of the Persian Empire and the coming of the brief empire under Alexander the Great and the Macedonian Greeks.

That remarkable empire stretched from Greece all the way to India, taking in all the old civilized lands. But the latter part of the prophecy is very important to us. It concerns events that transpired after Alexander's death in 323 BC and the resulting division of his conquered territories among his four strongest generals.

This division of the civilized world was extremely important. It resulted in extended conflicts and wars among those four sections of the known world. So as the centuries passed, there developed a continuing test of power between the old lands of civilization in Asia and the newly emerging civilizations on the European continent. Out of this situation, there emerged two mighty centers of power that God described for us in this prophecy as *the King of the North and the King of the South.*

Historically, this condition can be better understood as the ongoing struggle that has long existed between Europe and Asia. And it is still there today as seen in the extreme tensions that have continued between Christian Europe and America and the Islamic Middle East. We read in Daniel 11:40, "And at the time of the end the king of the South shall push at him."

This then is the time of the end. What does that mean? Is it the end of the world? Well, there are various "ends" in the Word of God, but this one has to do with the end of the entire age of man and the governments of man. This is the end that everyone talks about. And it is also the time of the last conflict and push that would take place between Europe and Asia, which are the domains of these "kings" of the North and of the South.

If this is the case—and this time of the end is now closing in upon us in our present generation—then this last conflict between Europe and Asia should be recognizable to us as something that has already happened or is about to happen in our own world.

As we read through chapters 11 and 12 of Daniel's prophecy, there are historical milestones that pop out. In 11:31, we can see the era of the Romans flashing by, and it is described by the same words, *abomination of desolation*, that are recorded in chapter 8. Then as we near verse 40, the Roman era ends and the period of European colonial power and military expansion begins. At that point, the modern world is upon us, far into the future from the time when Daniel lived.

> *And at the time of the end shall the king of the South push at him: and the king of the North shall come against him like a whirlwind, with chariots, and with horsemen, and with many ships, and he shall enter into the countries, and shall overflow and pass over.* (11:40)

The King of the South, at this late point in time, was the aging Ottoman Empire, headquartered in Turkey, and several centuries old at this point. It still held onto extensive regions stretching from the Adriatic Sea around the eastern end of the Mediterranean Sea and across part of Northern Africa. It was a vast empire that had been full of glory and immense power, but it was ready to fall. In fact, it was known at that time as the sick man of Europe.

WORLD WAR I

This pushing against Europe by the Ottoman Empire had been going on for quite a long time. But finally, in the year 1911, Europe began her last and victorious push back at them. The Italians seized Tripoli that year away from the Ottomans, and then during the next two years, the Balkan countries fought two short wars against them.

That marked the beginning of a world war. There were indeed many contributing factors to World War I, but this confrontation of ambitious European countries against the weakened Ottoman Empire can be seen as the greatest cause. As verse 40 states, Europe unleashed a great flood of military might against the South, and it overflowed everything in its path.

As the bloody contest erupted, Turkey, the head of the Ottoman Empire, joined Germany and the Central Powers for the cause of common defense as well as for common aggression. Then the entry of the United States into the war on the side of the King of the North (most of Europe except for the Central Powers) provided the deciding factor in tipping the balance of power against the King of the South. An interesting note is this: verse 40 mentions horses, and horses were actually used by the British in their Sinai and Palestinian campaigns. Next verse:

> "He shall enter also into the glorious land, and many countries shall be overthrown: but these shall escape out of his hand, even Moab, and the chief of the children of Ammon" (12:41).

The war progressed, and there was much action in the Middle East as well as in Europe. The British pushed from Suez up to Jerusalem and surrounded it by the war's end. After the hostilities were over, the British were given a mandate to control both Palestine and Transjordan (now called Jordan).

Thus, we see Britain, a king of the North, possessing the land of Israel, which is described here as the glorious land. That was the first time a Northern or European government had had possession of the land of Israel since the times of the Romans, except for some brief snatches of territory during the period of the crusades.

But the age of colonialism was almost over, and Britain did not want to keep and administer all these holdings. They quickly gave up Transjordan, giving them their independence. This newly created country of Transjordan contained the old territories of biblical Edom and Moab, as well as the ancient land of the Ammonites. In fact, their capital is today called Amman. Therefore, just as Daniel foresaw and verse 41 states, these lands escaped out of the hand of the king of the North when Britain gave them their independence.

> *He shall stretch forth his hand also upon the countries, and the land of Egypt shall not escape. But he shall have power over the treasures of gold and silver, and over all the precious things of Egypt; and the Libyans and Ethiopians shall be at his steps.* (11:42-43)

During the era of colonialism, various other European colonial powers had been feuding over possession of the North African countries. Algeria was "owned" by France and Libya by Italy. Egypt was ruled by Britain from 1882 until the time of World War II.

Although it is a subject of much debate today, colonial rule was good for these undeveloped countries in some ways. At the same time, however, the resources of the colonized countries were tapped and exported by the conquering powers. They definitely had power over their gold and silver, as the prophecy states.

THE FAR EAST

> *But tidings out of the East and out of the North shall trouble him; therefore he shall go forth with great fury to destroy, and utterly to make away many.* (11:44)

This language about the East seems to be a description of the scenario of World War II, which came not long after the first world war was ended (which was ironically called the war to end all wars). At that time, for the first time since the rampage of the Mongols under Genghis Khan, the Far East became embroiled in a major war with the European powers.

These tidings that came out of the East started with the devastating news about the Japanese attack upon Pearl Harbor, and it caused the assembling of the great Allied war effort in the Pacific.

Something unusual that can be seen in this passage by Daniel is that the King of the North (here the Allied powers) is troubled by tidings, which came out of their own territory in the North. This is what happened as from within the constantly troubled ranks of the European countries came a terrible internal threat and upheaval.

The tidings out of the North could well refer to the news about the onslaught of the German machine of war under the hand of Adolf Hitler. These forces swept across Poland in a heartbeat and then occupied the country of France with apparent ease.

But the power of Germany and their Axis allies stopped at the English Channel when Hitler paused his westward push and turned to invade Russia. Then the United States, who also qualifies as a King of the North, entered the war; and the tide turned against Germany, Japan, and their allied nations. The fury that was unleashed against Germany and Japan by the Allies was awesome, just as it is described by the language of verse 44. Nuclear weapons were used for the first time in history.

> *And he shall plant the tabernacles of his palace between the seas in the glorious holy mountain; yet he shall come to his end, and none shall help him.* (11:45)

After the fury and destruction was finished, the King(s) of the North did what victors always do, which was to expand the glory of their influence. The tabernacles that are seen in this verse are tents, buildings that are not primary or permanent structures. When we consider what these tabernacles of the palace (government) of the King of the North might be, we see tent structures that are extensions of the main building.

To the victors in war belong not only spoils but also the spread of their influence and cultures into conquered territories. This was also characteristic of the colonial system of rule. In every country that came under the dominion of a colonial power, extensions of the culture and government of the mother country were set up.

After World War II was over, the task of sorting out new national boundaries and forming new nations out of tattered countries had to be undertaken. One of the most important areas of concern was the land of Palestine. Britain was determined not to continue her possession of that land, so something had to be done.

The *glorious holy mountain* in verse 45 must refer to Israel and particularly Jerusalem with its famous temple mount. As far as being "between the seas" is concerned, that is exactly the description of that area of land. It is located at a point between the Dead Sea and the

Mediterranean, as well as the Sea of Galilee, not to mention the Persian Gulf and the Caspian Sea and Black Sea. One sees a confluence of seas in that part of the world.

After the war ended, the European powers, with the exception of Russia, had experienced quite enough of the trouble of trying to rule the world. Also at this point in history, the threat of possible global nuclear war was making a profound change in the old mentality of empire building. The vast colonial holdings around the world that had not already been given up by that time were fast escaping into the realm of their own national identity.

Britain, however, still had a very hot potato in her hands with her mandate over Palestine. So in 1948, through events that were definitely under God's control, the new nation of Israel was born and given the blessing of the Western Allies and the United Nations. Jews had already begun filtering back to Israel even before the war began. Now they came in earnest with a determination that captured the admiration and support of the whole Christian world—and the hatred of the Islamic world.

ISRAEL'S RETURN

From the very beginning, the new nation of Israel got the bulk of her support from the United States, and even today, they receive considerable aid from us. The men and women who have fashioned this prosperous nation out of a desolate and poverty-stricken land have migrated there mostly from Western nations. Therefore, the Israelites who were returning to their land were no longer the cultural children of the East.

The nation of Israel that is there now is essentially an island of Western culture that is surrounded by hostile Islamic countries, which not only hate their Jewish identity but also their Western ways and associations. So the peoples of Europe (America included) who are identified here as King of the North have extended the tabernacle of their palace even to the glorious holy mountain.

But verse 45 also says that the King of the North would come to his end, and none would help him. This is true in two ways. First, the colonial empires are almost gone. Britain has remaining only a commonwealth of countries sometimes called an old boys club.

Secondly, even though the King of the North became victorious over the southern regions as the result of these two major wars, he also shall ultimately come to the place of losing total authority of even his own national dominion.

And the same shall be true of all the rest of the countries of the world. That is because King Jesus Christ shall descend from heaven and assume his rightful rule over all the dominions of the whole earth. At that time, as Habakkuk says, "The earth shall be filled with the knowledge of the glory of the Lord, as the waters cover the sea" (2:14).

Here Daniel's chapter 11 ends, but the vision continues through chapter 12.

> *And at that time shall Michael stand up, the great prince who stands for the children of your people, and there shall be a time of trouble, such as never was since there was a nation even to that same time: and at that time shall your people be delivered, every one that shall be found written in the book.* (12:1)

Michael appears to be God's chief angel of war, and because of the above statement, it may be that he is the special protector angel for Israel. It may well be that he actually did stand up in the year 1948 when Israel became a nation again. He has most certainly stood up for them during their fierce wars with the Islamic nations.

The time of trouble that is mentioned here has probably already started. It could be understood to be the time of horrendous world wars during the twentieth century, not to mention the nuclear standoff under which most of the population of our world has grown up. Historically, the twentieth century qualifies as the bloodiest and most war-torn century of all time. And there is likely much more violence to come before the Lord returns.

The above verse ends with the statement that those who are of Daniel's people will be delivered—who are found written in "the book." Any effort to interpret this statement would have to be theological and certainly controversial.

It may be that the angel has reference to the recent gathering of Israelites from out of the nations of the world in order for them to become the new citizens of Israel as we now know Israel in our time. They were delivered from the wars of the twentieth century as well as from the many persecutions that have been the lot of Jewish people in most of the countries where they have lived. And some of them were delivered from the Nazi Holocaust. While others died, those were delivered and gathered to become the end-time nation of Israel. When more trouble and persecution arises, there will always be more deliverance.

The "book" mentioned in chapter 12, verse 1, seems to be the Lamb's Book of Life in which the names of all the eternally redeemed people of all nations and of all time are written. It was written and finished before the world began as shown in Revelation 17:8. Finally, jumping far ahead in time, after the thousand year reign of Christ with his chosen people is over, that book will be opened and names checked to see who is in there. (God always knows, but this is for the human record.) This is seen in Revelation 20:12-15.

The next verse in chapter 12 brings in the resurrection of the people of God and the beginning of the millennial age. (You should be reading this with your Bible in hand.) Therefore, when the events of chapter 11, just described, are over, Christ will be ready to make his grand entrance. So time is fast running out.

CHAPTER 3

In the Days of These Kings...

When I was a young man of about twenty, our pastor preached a sermon I shall never forget. It was from the second chapter of Daniel. What I learned from that message anchored my faith in the God who exists just as our Bibles describe him. He is not pantheistic, and he is not an unknowable force. He knows and directs the events of the future and tells them to his prophets before they ever start to happen. Fulfilled prophecy absolutely clinches just who he is. I especially needed that knowledge and assurance at the time, and now I love to share the message with others who have the same need.

Something else we learn from this prophetic message in Daniel is that the timing of Christ's return to the earth will be in conjunction with the appearance of certain great national governments. So let us see if those governments that he described are here with us today. If they are, then we can anticipate that our redemption is drawing near.

THE SETTING

In the sixth century before the birth of Christ, the people of Israel were in their forced captivity in the country of Babylon. They had been carried there by the powerful army of the Babylonian emperor, Nebuchadnezzar, because their accumulated sins had finally exhausted God's long-suffering. But while they were in captivity, God placed his prophetic calling upon the young Israelite, Daniel, and gave him some wonderful visions about the future.

Chapter 2 of the Book of Daniel contains the account of a dream that King Nebuchadnezzar had one night which powerfully affected him, even though he could not remember what it was about. So he called in his staff of prophets and wise men to recall the dream for him and to interpret its meaning. After much failure on their part, the Hebrew Daniel finally arrived at the court among the other advisors. He and his friends promptly prayed for the answer, and God gave him the same detailed dream that Nebuchadnezzar had. By the Bible's own chronology, the year was 524 BC. This dream had a purpose, and in his interpretation, Daniel stated that God was showing to the king things that would be coming to pass in the latter days.

In his dream the king saw a great image that was made of several different materials. The head was gold, the chest and arms were silver, the stomach brass, the legs iron; and the feet were made of a mixture of iron and clay. Daniel told the king that his great government of Babylon was represented by the head of gold.

The interpretation that God gave to Daniel went on to show that this magnificent image represented the passage of time, beginning with the head and progressing downward to the feet. Daniel also was shown that each of the different materials of which the image was made represented powerful world-class empires that would be successively rising and falling through time after the empire of Babylon was ended.

To many readers of the Bible, this is only so much dry, ancient history. However, our interest in these bygone events can suddenly perk up when we realize that they can tell us a lot about our own time and where we ourselves stand in God's prophetic plan.

THE MEANING OF THE IMAGE

Bible commentators are generally agreed about the meaning and application of the materials that made up the image. The head of gold represented the great shining Babylonian empire. After that fact is understood it is not difficult to see how the other materials correspond directly to several world empires that arose and fell after Babylon was fallen and gone.

Next came the Medo-Persian Empire, represented by the metal silver, whose army entered and took the formidable city fortress of Babylon on the night of Belshazzar's feast (Daniel 5). In time, after the Persian Empire declined, it was conquered by a rising power from northern Greece. This was represented in Nebuchadnezzar's dream image by the belly and thighs of brass. Then in 323 BC, this Greek Empire of Alexander the Great came to its end when that great conqueror died.

This is the point when the Romans entered the picture, it being generally agreed that the Roman Empire is represented by the legs of iron which were below the thighs of brass. And the two iron legs may show symbolically how the Roman Empire became divided into its Eastern and Western divisions.

In the year AD 800 the old, decayed Roman Empire was given new life under a new emperor named Charlemagne, and it came to be called the *Holy Roman Empire*. But nationalism, as we know it today, slowly began to sprout within the vast lands of the empire, and different regions of the European continent started to seek more independence both from the empire and from the Roman Catholic Church.

THE END OF ROME

Finally, the competition between the archaic empire system and the emerging independent states of Europe came to a final head in the year 1648 with the Treaty of Westphalia, the last major treaty to be drawn up in Latin, the language of the Romans. The time of the legs of iron on Nebuchadnezzar's image had finally ended. It was not that people were tired of the idea of world empire or that the dream of having one world government was dead. It certainly is not dead today. But the time had come when realities in the western part of the world had greatly changed. Columbus had already accomplished his voyages to the New World by that time, and the Portuguese had discovered how to sail around the tip of Africa to the Orient.

The whole American continent, Africa, and all the Middle and Far East were up for grabs. The great race that pitted each European state against the others to see which one could claim the greatest part of the newly discovered world had started. For the next three hundred years, the world witnessed the art of empire building being developed to its greatest peak in history. We now call it *the colonial period*.

THE LAST AGE OF EMPIRE

How much of the world was affected by the building of these huge colonial empires? Well, the whole of the American continent was carved up primarily by Spain, Portugal, England, and France. Almost all of

Africa was gobbled by Britain, France, Germany, Portugal, and Italy. Britain also got Australia, India, and parts of the Orient. And on and on it went.

Now how does this historic phenomenon fit into King Nebuchadnezzar's prophetic dream? Historically, the legs of iron that were part of his dream image ended with the death of the Roman Empire system in 1648. The next and last part that made up the image was the feet and toes, which were made of a mixture of iron and clay. What do we have here? The iron clearly represents the very hard and durable spirit of conquest and rule that was the backbone of the great Roman experience—the dream to rule the world.

Symbolically, the iron appears again in the feet and toes that we see here representing the colonial era of world history. The iron was left over from Rome, and it endured within Europe, which is the very geographic area that had made up the bulk of the Roman Empire. This iron was essentially the tenacious will and desire that remained in the hearts of the European people to rule as the Romans had ruled.

BUT THE CLAY

However, by this point in time, a new element had entered the picture. It was the equally intense desire on the part of every one of the emerging European nations to keep their own independence separate from the other states. We call it *nationalism*. Therefore, this conflict of ideals that existed between the strong iron and the brittle clay set the scene for three hundred years of bloody conflict that saw one European nation after another trying to grab all the world it could get, just as the Romans had done, but none willing to be under subjection to any other.

Some of the notable efforts at reforging the iron of empire were made by the country of France under Louis XIV and later under Napoleon, also by Germany during World War I under the kaiser (*kaiser* means "caesar" in German) and Hitler during World War II. The Russian word *czar* also means "caesar," and the czars played their important part in the fray. Russia's greatest effort at making world empire was, however, under their communist regime during the Cold War.

It was a glorious time for the many conquering nations while it lasted, but the colonial period has presently almost run its course. There are not many colonial possessions left in the world now. Since World War II, the ensuing Cold War, and nuclear stand-off, the major powers of the world have generally conceded that this game has become too dangerous to play. Russia did, of course, extend their efforts to rule the world up until about 1990.

THE EMPIRE OF CHRIST

Before this colonial era will have completely ended, God has made it clear that one more empire will be forming and will break suddenly into the historic picture. It will not be an empire of man's making, and it was not even represented in the panorama of empires that were displayed in the image that King Nebuchadnezzar saw.

After the king had finished viewing the image that was before him, he saw something remarkable. He saw a stone that was cut out without hands which came to the image, struck it upon its feet of iron and clay, and broke them all to pieces. The entire image was shattered and destroyed while the stone grew into a great mountain and filled the whole earth. God gave Daniel the interpretation of this part of the dream also. Here it is in verse 44:

> *And in the days of these kings shall the God of heaven set up a kingdom, which shall never be destroyed: and the kingdom shall not be left to other people, but it shall break in pieces and consume all these kingdoms, and it shall stand forever.*

It is clear that the phrase "in the days of these kings" does not refer to all the kingdoms represented by the image because they ruled successively one after the other. It is important to note that the stone struck only one part of the image—the feet—and that was the period of colonialism.

We see pictured in this great shattering stone the entrance of the millennial kingdom of the Lord Jesus Christ. He is coming, and he will reign together with his saints over this whole planet that we live on—as is shown in Daniel 7:13-14. That world empire of Christ will last for a thousand years as stated in Revelation 20:4.

After that, the ungodly will be judged at the great white throne and consigned to a lake of fire forever. Then there will be revealed a new heaven and a new earth as shown in Revelation 21:1, and after that, Christ and his saints will still be reigning. It will never end!

So there is not much time left. The age of iron and clay is not quite finished, but it seems to be very close to its end.

CHAPTER 4

Power Groups at the End of Time

It should not seem strange to a Bible reader that the finish of our present world system should be described in detail by God's prophets. Several of the prophets in the Bible mention the end of the present world as we know it and the beginning of an entirely new age under the direct rule of the Lord Jesus Christ. The Book of Revelation gives the most information about these final things, but the Old Testament prophet Daniel was the one who recorded more than anyone else about events leading up to the actual return of the Lord. Here is what he wrote.

ON THE BEACH

> *In the first year of Belshazzar king of Babylon Daniel had a dream and visions of his head upon his bed. Then he wrote the dream, and told the sum of the matters. Daniel spoke and said, "I saw in my vision by night, and, behold, the four winds of the heaven strove upon the great sea. And four great beasts came up from the sea, diverse one from another."* (Daniel 7:1-3)

Daniel wrote this prophecy more than four hundred years before the birth of Christ. In his vision, he saw four animal forms rising out of the sea one after another. The meaning of the vision centers around the identity of these forms, the order in which they emerge and the things that happen to them after they come up. It is clear that the beasts symbolically represent governments that were yet to come into being when Daniel wrote this vision.

> *I Daniel was grieved in my spirit in the midst of my body, and the visions of my head troubled me. I came near unto one of them that stood by, and asked him the truth of all this. So he told me, and made me know the interpretation of the thing. These great beasts, which are four, are four kings, which shall arise out of the earth.* (Daniel 7:15-17)

In ancient times, governments and kings were the same thing. Governmental power and process were centered in kings, whereas today, for the most part, our governments are centered on a broader base involving congresses and parliaments. So "kings" in our modern times means governments and the nations over which they rule. Many Bible commentators have applied this chapter to the times of the ancient empires of the Old Testament, and that interpretation was the best they could offer with the information that was available to them long ago. We have more available today.

In our time, there are two good reasons for considering a modern application of this prophecy rather than one applied to ancient times. One reason is that nations are now existing on the world scene that more nearly fit Daniel's vision than the ancient empires ever did. Another reason is that the vision is actually dated for us if we read carefully. Of all the details that Daniel saw, the main event was the return to earth of Jesus Christ, called the Son of Man—which was a name he called himself. This has to be his second coming because his first coming, almost two thousand years ago, was not like not like the events that Daniel saw in this vision.

> *I saw in the night visions, and behold, One like the Son of Man came with the clouds of heaven, and came to the Ancient of Days, and they brought Him near before Him. And there was given Him dominion, and glory, and a kingdom, that all people, nations, and languages, should serve Him. His dominion is an everlasting dominion, which shall not pass away, and His kingdom that which shall not be destroyed.* (Daniel 7:13-14)

What this prophet of God was observing in this vision was the exact emergence and structure of world powers that would exist at the very end-time—the time of the coming of Christ to raise the dead. At that time, our Lord Jesus Christ will assume his rightful rule over all nations and will begin his thousand-year reign over all the earth. See Revelation 19:15.

Daniel could not have been aware of the meaning of all that he saw. He admitted that he did not understand many of the things that God showed him. And as much as man loves to predict the future, no one else could have known the identity of these four beasts until the time came when they actually would make their appearance up out of the sea of humanity.

Therefore, among the many advantages that have come to us who now live in the twenty-first century, this is one of them. And seeing the ancient prophecies coming to pass before our eyes gives a tremendous surge to our faith—or it should. Christ said, "And now I have told you before it come to pass, that, when it is come to pass, you might believe" (John 14:29). And that, by the way, is what Christ says is the reason for our having prophecy of future events in our Bibles. It is not for the purpose of telling the future in detail, but rather for recognizing the present and past events, which God has said would take place on the earth. And the purpose of it all is to aid our belief in the God who knows the end from the beginning.

So what about world power centers that will be in existence at the end of time? Are they on the world scene now? If they are, can we recognize them? Are they also described by the Lord's prophets? And does this vision of Daniel's have any connection to our present world order of things? If it does, then we will know that the millennial Sabbath will soon be here.

Now here is how Daniel saw the beasts (animal shapes) that arose out of the sea of the world's masses of people:

> *The first was like a lion, and had eagle's wings: I beheld till the wings thereof were plucked, and it was lifted up from the earth, and made stand upon the feet as a man, and a man's heart was given to it.* (Daniel 7:4)

Much of Bible prophecy is written in code. Even today, important governmental messages that are not meant to be seen by an enemy are often coded, and each code has its own symbols that must be deciphered for a message to be understood. The Lord Jesus himself put many of his messages in a code form called parables, in order to confuse the enemy. We readily see this in Matthew 13:10-17. But the symbols that are in prophecy are not always difficult to decipher. Many of the symbols in Revelation are given to us in the Old Testament if we take the time to look for them. Also, a fair understanding of world history is necessary for one to interpret Bible prophecies, or else how would he know whether a prophesied happening has ever been fulfilled or not?

As Daniel watched this first animal shape emerge out of the sea, he was seeing the formation of a governmental force whose symbol would be the *lion* and also the *eagle*. We know that in past history both of these symbols have been used to represent more than one country. But in this last age of time—which is the setting of this vision—there would be one outstanding power center that would use the two symbols in combination together—not just the lion, but the eagle as well.

BRITAIN AND AMERICA

The lion is the symbol of Great Britain today. This was the first animal form that Daniel saw emerging from the sea of humanity, and the order of this appearance is very important. Britain's power on the world scene dates at least from the time of their victory over Spain's great armada in 1588. Her vast colonial empire began to grow very fast after that, and by the twentieth century, there was finally accumulated the largest land empire around the globe that the world has ever seen.

But we notice that the lion has the wings of an eagle. We all know that the eagle is the symbol of the United States, which was Britain's chief colonial possession during her early empire period. Now that Britain has lost most of her colonial empire, this loss of power and standing is more than made up for by the huge power and status of the United States. Now the entire English-speaking world, which makes up a large part of the world's population, follows the lead of the United States and the heritage that came through Britain.

The plucking of the wings that Daniel saw could mean a number of things. There did come the actual separation of our two countries when America won its independence. Or it may mean that the world expansion of the English-speaking nations has ceased, which has happened with the near decease of colonialism.

Whatever it means, it has to do with the lion standing upon its feet as a man and a man's heart being given to it. This is a remarkable statement, and it fits perfectly. The other beasts we see in this chapter are "beasts" purely and simply, but this first one becomes as different from them just as a man is different from an animal.

America and Britain have long been the main center of Protestant Christianity in the world, and our Christian ethics affect our international policies and actions. America is known for giving away its wealth rather than for conquering and stealing. The Bible speaks of a new heart that is given to those who are born of God, and this heart differs from the stony cold heart of humanism. This is why America and Britain have been the most compassionate and unselfish of all recent nations.

THE RUSSIAN BEAR

> *And behold another beast, a second, like to a bear, and it raised up itself on one side, and it had three ribs in the mouth of it between the teeth of it, and they said thus unto it, Arise, devour much flesh.*
> (Daniel 7:5)

It is well known that the bear is the symbol of Russia today. She began her period of empire building only shortly after the rest of Europe made its start. But Russia lagged well behind the others and was not much of a world force to be reckoned with until after Peter the Great came to power in the late 1600s. He forcefully westernized his backward nation and set it well on the road to greatness. Her status as a superpower, however, began only in the twentieth century and especially since World War II. She became a world superpower after the United States had already attained that status. So the bear arose after the lion and the eagle.

As Daniel observed this bear, it was in an unusual position. It was apparently straining itself to one side and grasping three of its own ribs between its teeth. What could this mean? Well, the country of Russia lies geographically between Europe and Asia, and it contains elements of both continents and civilizations. Russia's desire to expand toward the East has long been stopped because of the presence and power of the great nation of China. But her drive at building an empire has been better satisfied by her push westward so that she has been enabled to fulfill the command that Daniel heard being given to her, "Arise and devour much flesh."

The three ribs forcefully held between the teeth of the bear bring to mind the countries of Eastern Europe that fell under Russia's domination after World War II. So we see the great bear lunging westward, just on one side, to devour everything it could. But why the three ribs? The number

3 is connected with one of the most basic numbers in Bible prophecy, and that is the fact that Europe's symbolic number in the Bible is 10.

Since nationalism began to grow on the European continent after the Renaissance, there have generally been ten nations that have emerged out of the Holy Roman Empire that ruled through the Middle Ages. Also, the number 10 applies to Europe in the sense that European languages come from ten separate roots, and language always plays an important part in the identity of countries.

The three ribs held in the teeth of the Russian bear appear to be three of these language groups, and the land area in which they are found takes in the countries of Eastern Europe. These are the countries that existed for many decades behind the iron curtain. They would have been free from the Russian bear if they could, but the bear was stronger than they were. And the bear still holds a strong influence over Eastern European countries today.

THE LEOPARD WITH FOUR HEADS

> *After this I beheld, and lo another, like a leopard, which had upon the back of it four wings of a fowl. The beast also had four heads, and dominion was given to it.* (Daniel 7:6)

One of the ways to recognize a power group in today's world is to observe and see who is making the most noise. Nations that tend to have prominence over others make a lot of commotion, and most of the uproar in our times is coming out of the Middle East.

Certainly, we do not see a unified effort at empire building there in the Middle East although Iran seems to have something like that in mind. But we do see much common cause and much unified policy, mostly directed against the West. There is also the existence of a fierce sort of nationalism, not only in the individual countries that make up that part of the world but also in the entire Arab world, and especially the Islamic World.

This form of a leopard is difficult to pin down. After all, it has four heads, and a leopard with only one head is dangerous enough. Obviously, there is no superpower in our present world whose symbol is the leopard, much less one with four heads. But the existence of the four heads indicates something to us, and that is that nobody is actually in charge. And interestingly enough, that is exactly the situation in the

Middle East today. These nations are all fiercely independent and yet are bound together by common ideals and goals, which include demolishing Israel if they can, thumbing their noses at the Western World, bleeding as much oil profit out of the Western World as they can—and establishing Islam as the world's one religion.

Plainly, the symbol for just one nation would not do at all to describe the Middle East. So the Lord seems to have given us a symbol that belongs to not just one nation in that part of the world but, actually, to all of them. And that symbol is the leopard. This is an animal whose natural habitat is the crescent that takes in the nations of Arab dominance—from North Africa into Asia. That is where true leopards live, not those in other parts of the world that are sometimes misnamed leopards.

Daniel's statement that dominion was given to this beast is interesting. All the other animals of this vision take their territory by their own power and force. That is the way in which countries usually come into world power. But in this case, the countries of North Africa and the Middle East have, for the most part, been given their independence and dominion by the colonial European powers that, at one time, had that part of the world under their control.

Most of this newfound dominion has been completed only since the second world war. So this fact also agrees with this animal's position of rising up out of the sea after the lion and bear had already emerged. Sequence is important here. The four heads on the leopard are difficult to identify. They may simply refer to the ancient peoples who have lived there for so long—such as Babylonians (Iraqis), Persians, Syrians, and Lebanese. However, the Arabs have come to dominate the whole area, and many of the Middle Eastern countries now speak forms of Arabic.

There is some time yet left, and things can change fast in that part of the world. But the truth is that the Arab world has become a definite power center and one that the superpowers have to reckon with constantly. According to Daniel's vision, it will remain one of the four major world forces until Jesus Christ the Redeemer comes and will likely become more forceful as time goes along.

THE BEAST OF WORLD EMPIRE

> *After this I saw in the night visions, and behold a fourth beast, dreadful and terrible, and strong exceedingly; and it had great iron*

> teeth. It devoured and broke in pieces, and stamped the residue with the feet of it. And it was diverse from all the beasts that were before it; and it had ten horns. (Daniel 7:7)

This last of the animal forms that came up out of the sea was not named. But this is not the only place this beast appears in prophecy, and we will glean more information about it from the Book of Revelation. There in chapter 13, the beast is shown to be a composite of other animal shapes, but the whole of its appearance is that of *a dragon.*

Revelation also tells us that it receives its power from the great red dragon, and the dragon is revealed in Revelation 12:9 as being Satan. Chapter 17 of Revelation also reveals much about the dragon and shows how it has operated in the world for many thousands of years. Its most important identifying mark is its seven heads with which it appears in the Revelation scriptures. In Daniel's vision, it apparently has only one head, but it also has ten horns just as it does in Revelation.

The beast does not have the same problem with its multiple heads as the leopard had, which we have just seen. The reason for that is that the seven heads have not all existed at the same time. They have grown on the animal one by one through the ages of time. When John, in Revelation, saw the beast, it was shown to him as it has evolved through long centuries of time, but Daniel's view of the beast takes in just the one period of time at the close of the age. By then, the other six heads on the beast have all come and gone. There was just one head left when Daniel saw it, and with it, the beast and the dragon were *making their very last stand.*

To understand this amazing beast, we must begin long ago. Before Abraham was born, Satan had succeeded in forming a great empire in Egypt that controlled the small civilized world at that time. This empire persecuted the Hebrews, the people of God, and kept them in slavery. There have been other world empires since Egypt, and almost all of them have had the characteristic of persecuting and even trying to annihilate the people of God—both Jews and Christians. Satan reveals his wicked hand every time these persecutions take place, and so it is not difficult to trace his tracks through the ages of time in this manner.

Let's look at the again. The seven great empires of world history correspond to the seven heads upon the beast that appears in Revelation and also in Daniel. And they are as follows:

1. Egypt, until the seventh century BC.
2. Assyria, sixth to seventh century BC.
3. Babylon, fifth century BC.
4. Persia, fourth century BC.
5. Greece, fourth century BC.
6. Rome, second century BC until the AD fifth century in the West and past that period in the East. It was revived in the West in AD 800 and continued until about 1650.
7. The colonial empires of Europe. These independent nations have carried on the search for world empire until the present time since 1650.

There are many characteristics about this beast in Daniel's vision that identify him. One is the iron teeth. God had already shown to Daniel the fact that great world empires would exist through time. The iron in the image in chapter two of Daniel's prophecy represented first the empire of Rome and then the European colonial nations afterward.

THE DRAGON'S LAST STAND

By the time this beast of world empire is seen rising to the surface of the sea along with the other power centers, it is operating under its last head, which represents the age of European colonial power. All the other empires and the six heads, which represented them, have vanished away by this time. The ten horns are all on this last head, and they further identify the beast because 10 is the number of Europe.

The nations of Europe are strongly independent of one another and have fought many wars over their colonial possessions in America, Africa, and the Far East. But they never had any problem in making temporary unions with one another in order to pursue grand military schemes to conquer the world. In chapter 2 of Daniel, Europe is pictured as the two feet upon a great image—feet that are made of a mixture of iron and clay. Just as iron and clay will not stick together, Europe is the same way, and it will be that way until the Lord comes.

This beast, as Daniel was seeing, trampled upon everything that was before it—as every world empire has done. In verse 23, we see that it devours the whole earth. And that is just what these particular empires have done, time after time, conquering all the civilized worlds that were known to them. This took place long before Britain, Russia, and the Near East came into their present positions of world power. Therefore, in order to bring this last beast up-to-date and place it properly in relationship with the other beasts, the Lord supplies us with another factor to consider.

THE "BIG" LITTLE HORN

> *I considered the horns, and, behold, there came up among them another little horn, before whom there were three of the first horns plucked up by the roots. And, behold, in this horn were eyes like the eyes of a man, and a mouth speaking great things.* (Daniel 7:8)

As Daniel was watching, an eleventh horn came up among the other ten and ripped up three of the ten by their roots. The *eyes of a man* in this little horn indicate that this is man's work, which it is doing, and not God's work. Briefly, the picture we are given here is of another national force that invades Europe, captures three of its language divisions, and promotes new things—new philosophies that are man centered. Today, this philosophy is called, among other things, humanism, and it has been the core philosophy of the world force of communism. We see more about this in verses 24 and 25.

> *And the ten horns out of his kingdom are ten kings that shall arise. And another shall arise after them, and he shall be diverse from the first, and he shall subdue three kings. And he shall speak great words against the Most High, and shall wear out the saints of the Most High, and think to change times and laws. And they shall be given into his hand until a time and times and the dividing of time.*

Here is the ambitious little horn, trying for all it is worth to become a big horn. It even aspires to become an eighth head upon the beast of world empire as seen in Revelation 17:11. But time is running out, and God says there will be only seven heads on the beast and no more. The eighth attempt would be a failure. Therefore, this edict is stated in the next verse:

> *But the judgment shall sit, and they shall take away his dominion, to consume and destroy it unto the end.*

Satan never runs out of plans and tricks, and if the last or seventh head cannot be reformed into a powerful eighth one, then he will nevertheless break out somewhere. So the vision shows an eleventh horn coming up among the ten and then beginning a fight for domination of everything around it, just like old times. In the process, the new horn rips up three of the other horns by the roots. So we see a pattern.

The ten horns, of course, are the (generally) ten nations of Europe in the last days. Another strong force, the eleventh horn, was prophesied to arise among these nations and do great damage. *And this is the point in time at which this fourth beast arises out of the sea of humanity and presents itself to Daniel's observation.* This little horn began its rise to power during the time between the two world wars, when European colonialism was declining. A powerful new force began to arise in Europe. It was the Marxist communist world revolution. This social and political revolution was similar to the French Revolution in that it squarely attacked Christianity. It also sought to revolutionize the social structure of the Western World.

As Daniel watched and listened, it came forth speaking "great things." It dedicated itself to the conquest of the world, and in this manner, Satan's try at forming an eighth head on his old beast of world empire got under way. This eleventh horn was his last political and military effort to consolidate the governments of man under his control, and this last attempt began with the communist world revolution and a long Cold War.

Satan uses social crusades and movements only so long as they suit his purposes. Communism has been useful to him in that it has instilled the discipline of obedience to authoritative power in the minds of a great number of people.

Now as the twentieth century has closed, the greater part of this fantastic communist empire has suddenly fallen apart almost as if on command. The Cold War is over. Russia is now "friends" with the USA and the other "Christian" nations of the world. China and a few other countries still hold to the ideals and concepts of the communist revolution, but with the fall of the iron curtain in Europe, the whole Western World is breathing much easier.

What will be happening next? The world's experience thus far with godless humanism and the communist revolution has done much to reveal the differences between those who love God and those who hate him. We do know that the beast of world empire will be destroyed, as stated in verse 11, and the destruction process may be unfolding in these times before our eyes.

> *I beheld then, because of the voice of the great words which the horn spoke; I beheld even till the beast was slain, and his body destroyed, and given to the burning flame.*

This slaying of the beast does not necessarily mean that the nations that were supporting his drive for world empire would all be destroyed. It appears from scripture that the beast is actually the name of a demonic spirit of extra high degree, positioned just under the ruling office that belongs to Satan himself. And there is one other powerful spirit in this same class, and he is called the false prophet. Revelation 19:20 shows both of them being cast into the lake of fire, which is the second death. It may be that this event will happen even before the advent of our Lord. In fact, it may already have happened. But that is another subject.

THE NEW DOMINION

> *I beheld till the thrones were cast down, and the Ancient of Days did sit, whose garment was white as snow, and the hair of His head like the pure wool. His throne was like the fiery flame, and His wheels as burning fire. A fiery stream issued and came forth from before Him. Thousand thousands ministered unto Him, and ten thousand times ten thousand stood before Him. The judgment was set, and the books were opened.* (Daniel 7:9)

The fulfillment of this prophesy will undoubtedly be the coming of the Lord God the Father, also the resurrection of the people of God and the putting down of all earthly powers. There are many scriptures through the Old and New Testaments that speak of this event, each of them in its own way. Here the awesome aspect of the occasion is emphasized as well as the effect it will have upon the nations of the earth when it happens.

The Ancient of Days is apparently God the Father. On this occasion, his coming down to the earth will be more awesome than when he came down upon Mt. Sinai with great displays of power and glory as seen in Exodus 19. He has promised his Son that he will make his enemies his footstool (Psalm 110:1 and Hebrews 1:13), so the first thing that we observe is that the thrones, or governments of these world power centers, will be cast down.

The judgment that is mentioned is not the final judgment of the unbelievers that is vividly described in Revelation 20. That event will happen at the end of the thousand-year reign of Christ. But this will be the beginning of Christ's reign with his church, and it will be a reign of judgment through and by the saints of God, directly under the rule of Christ Jesus, the King of kings (I Corinthians 6:2 and Revelation 3:21). Paul told us that we saints would even be judging angels.

Also from this verse above, we can deduct that as the One who is the Ancient of Days descends, there will be a tremendous display of power, accompanied by awesome fire and the appearance of the same "wheels" that Ezekiel described in the first chapter of his prophecy. We are also told what will happen to the great power centers and the rest of the nations of the world when God the Father and Jesus Christ arrive to this earth.

> *As concerning the rest of the beasts, they had their dominion taken away; yet their lives were prolonged or a season and time.* (Daniel 7:12)

The nations that had been leading the three great power centers (the lion, bear, and leopard) will be preserved to continue through the reign of Christ, but under his rule. The rest of the nations will be preserved in some form also, through the thousand-year reign.

THE SON ARRIVES

Next, we see in verses 13 and 14 of Daniel's prophecy the appearance of the Son:

> *I saw in the night visions and behold, one like the Son of Man came with the clouds of heaven, and came to the Ancient of Days, and they brought Him near before Him. And there was given Him dominion and glory and a kingdom, that all people, nations and languages should serve Him . . . an everlasting dominion which shall not pass away.*

So at this point, the Son of God arrives to take over the control of the earth from the Father. And the unique thing about his reign is that it will never end. All other kingdoms and empires have always come to an end, but this one never will.

And notice that he comes *in the clouds of heaven*. Why clouds? Because that will be part of the identity of his coming. He is the One who will come in the clouds. He was on this world once before you know, born of a mother and growing up to manhood. It won't happen that way again. He is coming straight from heaven, and when he enters this world's atmosphere, he will make his appearance in clouds. That is the way he left this earth, written about in Acts 1:9-11:

> *And when He had spoken these things, while they beheld, He was taken up, and a cloud received Him out of their sight. And while they looked steadfastly toward heaven, behold two men stood by them in white apparel which also said, You men of Galilee, why do you stand gazing up into heaven? This same Jesus which is taken up from you into heaven shall so come in like manner as you have seen Him go into heaven.*

So *he comes with clouds*, and we who believe and are born from above will be with him there in the clouds of the sky before he ever touches the earth, as it reads in I Thessalonians 4:17, "Then we which are alive and remain will be caught up together with them [the resurrected dead in Christ] in the clouds to meet the Lord in the air. And so shall we ever be with the Lord." What a joy that will be for us who love the Lord. But for others, it will be not so joyful.

> *Behold, He comes with clouds, and every eye shall see Him, and they also which pierced Him, and all kindreds of the earth shall wail because of Him. Even so, Amen.* (Revelation 1:7)

But there is more in this seventh chapter of Daniel. We read in verse 27:

> *And the kingdom and dominion and the greatness of the kingdom under the whole heaven shall be given to the people of the saints of the Most High, whose kingdom is an everlasting kingdom, and all dominions shall serve and obey Him.*

The children of God (saints) reigning with Christ in the coming kingdom is a truth that is well documented in scripture. Revelation

5:10 tells us: "And has made us unto our God kings and priests, and we shall reign on the earth." Then 20:4 states, "And they lived and reigned with Christ a thousand years." And Matthew 5:5 tells us, "Blessed are the meek, for they shall inherit the earth."

But a very remarkable scripture about this is Revelation 3:21, the words of Christ: "To him who overcomes will I grant to sit with Me in My throne, even as I overcame and have sat down with My Father in His throne."

This statement by our Lord Jesus to one of the churches of Asia (and to us Christian overcomers today as well) explains a lot. Psalm 110:1 shows us Jesus Christ as he returned back to heaven and was seated on the right hand of God the Father—not actually on his throne, but at the side of it. The man Jesus Christ has been situated in that place now for about two thousand years, working at interceding to the Father on behalf of his children.

In the same manner, we children of God, after we are resurrected or changed, will be at the side of King Jesus doing his bidding as well. This is a prospect to look forward to—government service in the Kingdom of Jesus Christ. Can there be any better prospect than our serving the King Jesus who died for us and who bought us with the price of his own life's blood?

Perhaps you may have been of the view that Jesus is already on his throne. As far as we believers are concerned, he is on the thrones of our hearts. But the angel told his mother, Mary, that this child would sit upon the throne of his father, David (Luke 1:31-33). And that throne will come to rule over the whole world. The Bible teaches us that, someday, every knee shall bow and every tongue shall confess him as Lord. That's the whole world—children of God and children of the devil alike.

But the timing is important, of course. So Matthew 25:31 tells us when it shall begin. "When the Son of Man shall come in His glory and all the holy angels with Him, then shall He sit upon the throne of His glory. And before Him shall be gathered all nations, and He shall separate them one from another, as a shepherd separates His sheep from the goats."

Paul wrote in First Corinthians 15, "Then comes the end, when He [Christ] shall have delivered up the Kingdom to God, even the Father, when he shall have put down all rule and all authority and power. For He must reign until He puts all enemies under His feet. The last enemy that shall be destroyed is death."

Now when will this scenario take place? This seems to be a description of his long forceful reign over the earth. After all, the scriptures tell us that he shall rule with a rod of iron (Revelation 19:15).

Although his Father will have put down all the ruling dominions of this earth before the reign begins, there must be an ongoing process throughout his reign of enforcing the righteous laws of God upon the earth. It may take a while for every knee to bow to the reigning King, but it will be done in process of time. Obviously, he will have to overcome tremendous resistance, but he will have the power to do that.

During this time, we children of God will be living in our glorified bodies that have been resurrected as we begin our reign with him. The rest of the world will apparently continue life as before, living and dying as generations will come and go. Then finally, all this will end with a final rebellion of man and the devil against God as pictured in Revelation 20:7-9 and the final destruction of all people who are not of God.

Daniel's great vision ended with a note of wonderful assurance for the saints of God. When Christ said, "Blessed are the meek, for they shall inherit the earth," he meant exactly what he said. So we see the family of God reigning jointly with Christ over the whole world:

> *And the kingdom and dominion and greatness of the kingdom under the whole heaven shall be given to the people of the saints of the most High, whose kingdom is an everlasting kingdom; and all dominions shall serve and obey Him.* (Daniel 7:27)

There is ample proof in Bible prophecy that this event will take place. So we see this major Bible prophecy about the arrangement of end-time powers winding down to its end in this our own time.

Chapter 5
The Four Horsemen of Revelation

From the beginning of time, man has been searching for ways to foretell his future and know his destiny. In ancient times, seers and prophets were highly respected for their art, and they often held positions of authority as advisors and counselors to kings.

For believers in God, however, there is only one way to reliably and safely learn about future events, and that is through the study and interpretation of Bible prophecy. The world of unbelievers knows little about the wealth of details about world affairs that is contained in the Word of God. Even Christians barely scratch the surface of the one-third of the Bible that is prophecy. But for those who do make a determined effort to search the prophets and who manage to get past the confusing problem of choosing interpretations, there is a mountain of gold in which to dig.

The Old Testament prophets foretold much about world affairs that were yet to come. There is disagreement, however, about the purpose of that primary New Testament prophetic work—the Book of Revelation. One view holds that it is only a symbolic representation of spiritual truths. Another says that it is truly prophecy of future events but that all these events took place within a period of just a few years after it was all written. Still, another states that its prophecies are all yet to come to pass and that they are reserved for a short seven-year span of time at the very end of our age. The most time-honored method of interpreting Revelation is that it was indeed future prophecy at the time it was written and that *it belongs to this whole age through which we are passing, which we call the age of the Gospel*. The prophesied events, however, are represented by symbols and they must be deciphered.

The Book of Revelation was written by the Apostle John, and he was also the writer of the Gospel book and the New Testament letters that bear his name. Revelation was the last of his writings, done when he was an old man in exile from the land of Israel. The first three chapters are the easiest to understand. They contain an initial vision of the Lord Jesus Christ, a statement about the purpose of the book, and Christ's instructions to the seven churches of Asia. The remainder of Revelation that follows chapter 3 contains the series of visions that God gave to John. This part is, by far, the most difficult scripture to understand in all the New Testament. There are many differing kinds of views about it that are held by Christians, and for this reason, it is easy for disagreements to occur.

WHY SYMBOLS?

A large part of the difficulty in interpreting Bible prophecy is the deciphering of its symbols. But if we should take a completely literal view and deny that there are symbols in prophecy, then we would have an even larger problem on our hands trying to explain just when and for what logical reasons such monstrous things as we read about in Revelation should ever occur. Sometimes, the writers of prophecy were struck dumb when they were confronted with the glory and majesty of God and the revelation of his mysteries. In fact, the prophets themselves did not always understand what they were seeing (see Daniel 8:27). Sometimes, a revelation from God was kept for a later time, usually the time when its fulfillment should finally come to pass (Daniel 12:9).

But the main reason why God used symbols in prophecy is the same reason why Christ used them in his parables. And that was to hide the meaning from unspiritual Godless inquirers. His statement in Matthew 13:10-16 explains this. The object is to keep people without spiritual understanding from finding out the plans and purposes that God has in store. God's people, on the other hand, can have this knowledge through the application of the Spirit and investigation of the Word.

Christ did explain some of the symbols that he used in the parables. And some symbols in prophecy are also explained. For instance, the four beasts in the seventh chapter of Daniel turn out to be not beasts or animals at all, but kings and governments that would arise out of the peoples of the earth. And the peoples of the earth are represented by another symbol, the sea, as explained in Revelation 17:15. Therefore, we must approach the prophecy of Christ much as we do the parables of Christ, looking for the hidden meaning that is put there for the spiritual and studious reader.

The Apostle John's visions began with a glorious view of the Son of God. He was the One who received the information from his Father and, in turn, passed it on to John through his angels. So Revelation contains the words of Christ. Let us begin.

> *The Revelation of Jesus Christ, which God gave unto him, to show unto his servants things which must shortly come to pass; and he sent and signified it by his angel unto his servant John. Who bare record of the word of God, and of the testimony of Jesus Christ, and of all things that he saw.* (Revelation 1:1 2)

Notice that it says in verse 1 that these are things which must *shortly* come to pass. This is a vastly important statement, and it means that these prophesied events have been happening at their appointed times for almost two thousand years now. Thus, they are not all reserved for some short period of calamity and agony just before the second coming of Christ.

The series of prophetic visions that John received begins in chapter 4. He looked and saw a door opened in heaven and heard a voice calling him to observe things in the future. Looking, he saw a sealed book delivered into the hands of Christ, who appeared in the symbolic forms of a lion and a lamb.

It should seem apparent that since John was to see events of future, and since the following two chapters (5 and 6) present the opening of a book, that the book itself would contain the record of those events. Therefore, the sounding of the seven trumpets—which occurs immediately after the book is opened—must be the symbolic contents of the book and the record of the future as John looked forward from his time toward our time.

The book, however, was sealed shut when John saw it, and there was much crying about the fact that there was no one found who was able to open it. This sealing harks back to the ancient use of personal seals that were placed upon correspondence, possessions, and even tombs. The important thing about sealing something was that no one should open it again except the one who had the authority to do so. That would be the owner whose identifying mark was there upon the seal.

Reading on in chapter 5, we find that John and the heavenly witnesses were much relieved when One finally came forward who bore the authority of the seals. His appearance as a slain lamb revealed the identity of that authority. It was the Lord Jesus Christ himself, who had bought all the redeemed host as well as their eternal destiny with the price of his own life's blood. Therefore, they sang the song about his worthiness that appears in verse 9.

Another thing about the practice of sealing things was that it kept them shut until the authority gave permission for them to be opened. This is illustrated by the way in which Christ opened the scriptures to his disciples after his resurrection. One of them said, "Did not our heart burn within us, while He talked with us by the way, and while He opened to us the scriptures" (Luke 24:32). The important need for this can be seen in the fact that for the preceding three years that they had been with him, their understanding of these same scriptures had been very limited.

We can draw the conclusion, therefore, that the opening of these seven seals has to do with the opening of the reader's understanding about the mysteries that are found in this book of prophecy. Without some knowledge of what the seals themselves stand for, the rest of the book will remain effectively closed to us, and no amount of speculation will crack it open. Some interpreters who have misapplied these seals as representing historical events have gone on to apply the rest of the prophecy of Revelation to end-time catastrophes that cannot be supported by history, current events, or the rest of the scriptures. What they have done was to go rushing off to war with imagined an antichrist without having first opening their orders and reading them.

The seals upon this Book of Revelation are like the paper jacket on a modern book that contains the title and some description of what the book is about. The seals that John saw, therefore, do not themselves prophesy anything about the future. But they do identify the book upon which they were placed, speak of Christ the author, present the issues, and give some reason for being of the book. To be more exact, the first four seals describe God's methods and devices that he uses in accomplishing the events of prophecy. The fifth, sixth, and seventh seals show the issues that are at stake in this age—a colorful cameo description of the most powerful action in the book and a beautiful view of the deepest feeling between the two principal characters: Jesus Christ and his church.

THE FIRST SEAL

> *And I saw when the Lamb opened one of the seals, and I heard as it were the noise of thunder, one of the four beasts saying, Come and see. And I saw, and behold a white horse, and he that sat on him had a bow. And a crown was given unto him, and he went forth conquering, and to conquer.* (6:1-2)

The first four of the seals are represented by four horses and riders. Since they signify God's methods and devices that he uses in his global works, we can ask what his most important and powerful device is. Without question, it is the witness of his Word. The Word of God is the sharpest instrument ever devised, and no man can stand before it. It is that flaming sword in the hands of the cherubim that keeps the way of the tree of life. In the opening verses of the Gospel of John, we have the testimony that the Word is Christ, and he appears vividly as such in Revelation 19:11 and 13: "And I saw heaven opened, and behold, a white horse; and He that sat upon him was called Faithful and True, and in righteousness He judges and makes war . . . and He was clothed with a vesture dipped in blood; and His name is called The Word of God."

The Word of God has an irresistible effect in the world. It has brought ruling empires to their knees and has instructed kings and rulers all through time as well as the humblest of souls. God himself has stated that "it shall accomplish that which I please, and it shall prosper in the thing whereto I sent it" (Isaiah 55:11).

One of the characteristics of that Word is that it cuts and divides. The men of Israel who were assembled on the Day of Pentecost were pricked in their hearts by it. Therefore, it is likened to swords and arrows that cut and pierce: "And He has made my mouth like a sharp sword; and in the shadow of His hand He has hid me, and made me a polished shaft; in His quiver has He hid me" (Isaiah 49:2).

And so as the Word of God is like swords and arrows, we see the rider upon the white horse with a bow in his hand for shooting the arrows of God's truth. They rain upon his enemies and disobedient children alike in the form of bitter but encouraging correction. They conquer and subdue the flesh and sin and exalt Jesus Christ as Lord of heaven and earth. Therefore, our Lord's first device is his Word of truth, represented by the first seal.

Some futurist scholars have chosen to emphasize the fact that whereas the rider has a bow, no mention is made of any arrows. The idea that is drawn from this is that this rider represents a great future antichrist and that although he will have weapons at his disposal, he will actually make conquests over nations using threats and flattery alone. But this is grasping at straws. The Bible says that Jacob had divided to his sons the spoil that he took away from the Amorites: "With my sword and with my bow." Obviously, he used arrows too although they are not specifically mentioned. It is taken for granted that they were present and that they were used.

THE SECOND SEAL

And there went out another horse that was red, and power was given to him that sat thereon to take peace from the earth, and that they should kill one another. And there was given unto him a great sword. (6:4)

Here the color of the horse is red, and red is the color that is used frequently in the Bible as a symbol of judgment in the shedding of blood. It is the tragic task of this horseman to create warfare among the nations of the world. Could this really be a device of God? The idea is popular today that God hates man's use of war and bloodshed and wishes that people would learn to settle their differences in a more peaceable manner. And in truth, God does hate war, but he often finds it necessary to use this device to correct the ways of man and bring his often-delayed vengeance upon the wicked.

During the time of national turmoil when Jeremiah lived, God spoke through his prophet, saying, "I am pained at My very heart; My heart makes a noise in Me; I cannot hold My peace, because You have heard, O My soul, the sound of the trumpet, the alarm of war . . . for My people are foolish, they have not known Me" (Jeremiah 4: 19, 22).

From the seventh to the third centuries before Christ, God sent waves of invading armies back and forth across the civilized world as his means of reckoning with the depravity and idolatry of that ancient time. The writings of the Old Testament prophets are full of these accounts. Many empires rose and fell at God's command during that age, and it was all according to much warning and prophecy he had given before it all began. A brief example is Jeremiah 25:31-33: "A noise shall come even to the ends of the earth, for the Lord has a controversy with the nations. He will plead with all flesh. He will give them that are wicked to the sword . . . and the slain of the Lord shall be at that day from one end of the earth even unto the other end of the earth."

There is ample evidence that the bloodshed and destruction of warfare do constitute a major device that God puts to use in His rule of the affairs of this world. And it is vividly described here in the account of the red horse.

THE THIRD SEAL

> *And when he had opened the third seal, I heard the third beast say, come and see. And I beheld, and lo a black horse, and he that sat on him had a pair of balances in his hand. And I heard a voice in the midst of the four beasts say, A measure of wheat for a penny, and three measures of barley for a penny, and see that you hurt not the oil and the wine.* (6:5-6)

The recent highly popular futurist interpretation of this black horse holds that it represents famine of a terrible magnitude. It is surprising that this idea could be so readily accepted when the very opposite picture is presented to us. First of all, the announcement is not made of any scarcity of goods at all, but rather the availability of them and the fact that they are up for sale. And in addition, the prices are not black market prices either but are, instead, at a level that is low, even by ancient Bible standards. They are actually lower than the rock bottom prices for which goods were sold when the glut of the Syrian booty was brought into the gate of Samaria (I Kings 7:1).

What the rider on the black horse is actually doing is selling the goods of the earth for money, using the scales that are in his hand. What price does God expect for his blessings? There many who come to the sale with holes in their pockets. King Belshazzar was such a man as he climaxed a reign of misrule and debauchery with one last drunken, idolatrous fling on the night that his empire of Babylon fell. The handwriting that had appeared on the plaster of the wall that night had made this accusation: "You are weighed in the balances and are found wanting" (Daniel 5:27). These balances were the same as those in the hands of the rider upon the black horse.

God is very reasonable about these matters, and he does not expect anything from us that we cannot give. If we lay up our talents in napkins, however, or bury them in the ground, we will have no one to blame but ourselves when the hard times come. The Lord says, "Come now, and let us reason together" (Isaiah 1:18), and the Apostle Paul adds his testimony when he says that faithful duty is our "reasonable service" (Romans 12:1). God reasons with us about our service and duty as individuals and as nations. Because of this, it is the third beast who introduces this seal to John, and he is the one with the face of a man. This is man's particular quality, his ability to reason things out.

God makes it plain to us in scripture that our food products and other blessings are really his, and that he is the One who gives them to us (Ezekiel 16:19). When the time comes that enough people in a nation forget this fact, then the ever-present balances tip against that country, and they can expect to begin losing some of the abundance that they had enjoyed. Every nation on record has done that, and this is the reason that the Bible gives for the short life expectancy of the governments of this world. Belshazzar's Babylonian was only one of many nations and empires that existed during that age when God's controversy with the nations was raging. All of them finally lost out in the weighing process, and the situation still continues to our own time.

We should make no mistake about it, for the Lord does not give away his stores of goods and power for nothing. The word has always gone out, "A measure of wheat for a penny," and only those countries that have delivered the price have received the goods. When the French statesman, de Toqueville, visited America during the nineteenth century, he wrote upon his return to France, "I sought for the greatness of America in her harbors and rivers, and fertile fields, and her mines and commerce. Not until I went into her churches and heard her pulpits aflame with righteousness did I understand the greatness of her power. America is great because she is good: and if America ever ceases to be good, America will cease to be great."

It would seem that anyone could read history and see the truth of this matter. But there are always those, many of whom are in positions of power, who think they can cheat on God's system and come out ahead. It cannot be done. His balances will always find us out. So we see the black horse as the one which delivers wealth, prominence, and power to nations. These are mostly national and international matters with which we are dealing in this book of prophecy. God has chosen certain countries and areas of the world to set the standard of righteousness before their fellows, and he has given them the necessary resources to carry out that obligation. It is to those that this black horse is sent because this is one of God's methods, the setting up of national powers and the judgment of them according to their great responsibilities.

CONSERVATION AND ECOLOGY

To the nations that God favors to enjoy his prosperity, the admonition is made, "See that you hurt not the oil and the wine." This is simply a warning for them to practice conservation. The Lord expects us to respect his goods and resources highly. One of the harsh rebukes that he gave Israel when he judged them was that they had polluted the land. Environmental pollution is bad enough, but God pointed out the worst there is, which is the shedding of righteous blood and physical and spiritual adultery. History continues to repeat itself.

THE FOURTH SEAL

> *And I looked, and behold a pale horse, and his name that sat on him was Death, and Hell followed with him. And power was given unto them over the fourth part of the earth, to kill with sword and with hunger and with death, and with the beasts of the earth.* (6:8)

This time, it is not necessary to interpret the identity of the horseman, for he is named. Death too is a device of God in that it is the penalty for sin and would be eternal in its duration were it not for the promise of the resurrection for God's children. Moreover, the scriptures are filled with instances of God's bringing death upon the wicked and righteous alike. Good King Josiah's death was a blessing in that it prevented his seeing the defeat and the captivity of the kingdom of Judah. Herod's death, on the other hand, was judgment against him for refusing to give proper glory to God.

The introduction of this dreadful seal is made by the fourth beast, which had the face of an eagle. This is part of the Gospel message too and illustrates the swift and sure nature of this ultimate judgment. When Christ foretold that Jerusalem would be destroyed by foreign armies, he ended by saying, "For wheresoever the carcass is, there will the eagles be gathered together" (Matthew 24:28). The Jewish historian Josephus tells us that over a million were slain in that terrible war.

And then as Death himself rides the pale horse, Hell follows after. Hell represents here simply a separation from God and his blessings. The word is translated from the Greek word *hades*, which generally means the "abode of the dead." There is much hairsplitting over the various words that are translated into *hell*, but all of them share the meaning of separation from God, whether temporary or eternal, and it is that broad meaning that must be implied here as Death and Hell are given power to do their work in a global manner.

The mission of these two is one that affects huge numbers of people—nations and continents—and is the very opposite, the negative image, of the black horse. Whereas it was black, this one is pale. Whereas the black carried wealth, power, and the protection of God, this one carries hunger, the ravages of conquest, and an ignorance of God with separation from him.

It is important to notice that they are sent into only a part of the earth. This is not because death is ever completely restricted, but rather that where hell goes, there death has its greatest work to do. Nations that are conquered in war always have heavy losses to bury, whether from swords, bullets, or the famine and disease that always accompany defeat on the battlefield. Also, countries that are the poorest and most backward have the highest mortality rates.

It is stated in Psalm 9:17, "The wicked shall be turned into hell, and all the nations that forget God." This is the hell that we see here following death, not a personal depository after an individual's death, but a national removal from the favor of God. We will see later that the black horse of abundance and the pale horse of death and hell ride in opposite directions as God exercises these devices over all the world.

It might seem strange that one of the weapons shown to be in Death's arsenal is the beasts of the earth. These beasts can not only be quite literal, but also symbolic. They may represent the formidable war machines that belong to the nations that God raises up to expand and conquer. Daniel saw beasts rising out of the sea and was told, "These great beasts, which are four, are four kings, which shall arise out of the earth" (Daniel 7:17). Wherever these beasts go there, the dead always lie, and there the spoil is taken as death and hell ride together through the world working the will of God as countries rise and fall according to his decree and unfaltering plan.

These are the four horsemen of God, displayed in vivid imagery for the benefit of those who are students of his works and grace. They appear in their four divisions all through the Bible, although in different forms. Zechariah speaks of them as "the four spirits of the heavens, which go forth from standing before the Lord of all the earth."

As they appear here in Revelation, they are simply announced and displayed, but they have no particular destination. The effects of their labors will be seen as the prophetic action begins to unfold. Here they are again, briefly described as follows:

1. *White horse*—representing the conquering influence of the Word of God
2. *Red horse*—the bloodshed and destruction of war as God's punishment for national sin
3. *Black horse*—God's gift of material abundance and power to those nations that he favors pertaining to righteousness
4. *Pale horse with hell following*—natural death and a separation of nations and peoples from prominence and prosperity

Chapter 6
Testing the Seals

Because of the very basic and representative nature of the information contained in the seals of Revelation, it is important at this point to put some of them to the test. We have seen that the *first four seals* are a representation of the methods and means that God uses to bring to pass world events. Therefore, an examination of some of those events should prove these devices for what they are.

We will not be using modern events in this test because that would be too controversial. Instead, we will see how an Old Testament prophet applied these four seals to some of the events surrounding his own time. *Remember that the Bible is always its own best interpreter.* Often, the mysteries that confront us when reading one part of the Bible can be explained by searching out other parts of the Word. In fact, many of the symbols that appear in Revelation also occur in the Old Testament.

Probably the most basic study about world events in all the Bible is found in Daniel, chapter 2. As we have already seen, it contains the record of a vision of world governments that extended from the time of ancient Babylon until our own modern times, and even until the second coming of our Lord. It is a miniature study of four ancient world ruling empires and the array of modern nations that evolved out of them. Later in Revelation, particularly in chapter 13, we will need an understanding of these matters.

THE GREAT CONTROVERSY

Daniel was a young man when he was carried with a large group of Hebrew captives to Babylon after Jerusalem was conquered. He lived a long life and had a marvelous series of visions that contain more information about the development of nations than the writings of any other Old Testament prophet. Daniel wrote this second chapter in the fifth century BC. All of what he wrote was future to his time, but most of it is in the past to us today.

The nation of Babylon, at that time, had succeeded in conquering and subjecting all the known civilized world. The maps in the back of your Bible may show this tremendous empire and the extent of its influence. It may not seem so large to us today, but it was the whole world to the people of that time. We use the word *empire* for a nation that rules over other nations and the term *world empire* for one that rules over all known civilized nations.

We have already studied some of the second chapter of Daniel, but now we need to see an overall view of that tumultuous era. Nebuchadnezzar was the monarch of this great Babylonian Empire. He possessed a high degree of military genius as well as political ability, and he masterfully consolidated the gains of his invincible armies. God chose this point in time to reveal to him, as well as to Daniel, the future course of the rise and fall of world governments until the end of time. Therefore, this chapter is very much a focal point for the rest of the prophecy of the Bible.

Verse 28 tells us that these foretold events belong to "the latter days." This is a general expression that means the times that would be coming. Verses 31 through 33 describe a unique and impressive visual aid that God would be using in the dream vision. It was an image of vast proportions, and its purpose was to teach things about coming events. Each part of the image had its own particular meaning, as we shall see.

> *You, O king, saw, and behold a great image. This great image, whose brightness was excellent, stood before you, and the form thereof was terrible. This image's head was of fine gold, his breast and his arms of silver, his belly and his thighs of brass, His legs of iron, his feet part of iron and part of clay. You saw until that a stone was cut out without hands, which smote the image upon his feet that were of iron and clay, and broke them to pieces. Then was the iron, the clay, the brass, the silver, and the gold, broken to pieces together, and became like the chaff of the summer threshing floors, and the wind carried them away, that no place was found for them. And the stone that smote the, image became a great mountain, and filled the whole earth.* (Daniel 2:31-33)

Verse 34 introduces the second object in the vision, which was a great stone that was "cut out without hands." Then in the succeeding verses, the action takes place as the stone strikes the image, the image disintegrates, and the stone grows to fill the whole world. In verse 37, God begins to give a limited interpretation of what the vision means. Immediately we see that the five materials of which the image was made represent governments and that the head of gold stood for the Babylonian Empire which ruled over the whole known world at that very time.

> *This is the dream, and we will tell the interpretation thereof before the king. You, O king, are a king of kings, for the God of heaven has given you a kingdom, power, and strength, and glory. And wheresoever the children of men dwell, the beasts of the field and the fowls of the heaven has he given unto your hand, and has made you ruler over them all. You are this head of gold.* (2:36-38)

Part of this dream revelation was bad news for Nebuchadnezzar and Babylon. Rulers like to believe that their governments will last on and on, but God was revealing that this one would not. There would be several more world empires after Babylon had fallen, as is shown in verses 39 through 43.

> *And after you shall arise another kingdom inferior to you, and another third kingdom of brass, which shall bear rule over all the earth. And the fourth kingdom shall be strong as iron, for as iron breaks in pieces and subdues all things, and as iron breaks all these, it shall break in pieces and bruise. And whereas you saw the feet and toes, part of potter's clay and part of iron, the kingdom shall be divided; but there shall be in it of the strength of the iron, forasmuch as you saw the iron mixed with miry clay. And as the toes of the feet were part of iron and part of clay, so the kingdom shall be partly strong and partly broken. And whereas you saw iron mixed with miry clay, they shall mingle themselves with the seed of men, but they shall not cleave to one another, even as iron is not mixed with clay.* (2:39-41)

God goes on in his interpretation to give some facts about the world governments that would come after Babylon. The silver empire would be inferior in some ways to Babylon. The brass empire would be even more worldwide in its influence. And the iron empire would be particularly strong and long lasting.

Babylon's rule ended in the year 460 BC. This occurred when the Medes and Persians captured the city of Babylon by a very remarkable military operation that ended on the night of Belshazzar's feast (Daniel 5:31). From that time onward, Media and Persia ruled all the known world until their empire also fell. And on and on it went.

Two other world empires had come and gone by that time. The Bible gives a lot of information about these early empires of Egypt and Assyria. All together there have been six world empires that have existed thus far in time. The last, the Roman Empire, gradually broke into what we know today as the nations of Europe, and there has not been another one since. Europe today, of course, is not an empire. However, it is included in this prophecy in Daniel 2.

In Nebuchadnezzar's dream image, the Roman Empire is represented by the two legs of iron in verses 33 and 40. But verses 41 through 43 speak of the times after the fall of Rome, and the feet and toes made of iron mixed with clay refer to the independent countries of Europe that grew out of the collapse of the Roman Empire. The ten toes are especially meaningful because there are ten basic language groups that make up the Europe of our age. Ever since the Roman Empire crumbled to pieces there have been rulers in that area of the world who have tried to remake it. Three well-known historical figures who tried it were Louis XIV and Napoleon of France and Hitler of Germany. And today, the European Common Market is striving for European unity, but it has not come politically.

These continued efforts are the results of the strength of the iron that has been left over from iron Rome, the last and greatest of all the empires. But there is also the weakness of the clay, which makes every attempt at building a new world empire crumble away through lack of cohesion. This is one of the most amazing occasions of the fulfillment of prophecy in the Bible.

The most important event that is revealed in this vision concerns the stone that was cut out without hands that struck and demolished the image. The stone is explained in verse 44. It is the kingdom of God. It is important to see that the stone struck the image on its feet and toes, which represent the age of European power after the passing of the Roman Empire. The empire is represented by the legs of iron. Therefore, the stone does not signify the first coming of Christ and the establishment of the age of the church as some folks assume. That began during the times of Rome. It rather shows us the second coming of our Lord and the millennial kingdom that will begin at that time, which will consume all governments of the world and place all the earth under the personal rule of Christ.

Now you see why this mighty prophecy in Daniel 2 is so basic. It gives us some tools that we can use to dig into other Bible prophecies that concern the rise and fall of nations.

HORSES AT REST

Now we will go to the prophecy of Zechariah, written during the age of the empire of Persia. Persia was the empire that came immediately after Babylon and was represented in the dream image by the breast and arms of silver.

Zechariah 1:1-3: *"In the eighth month, in the second year of Darius, came the word of the Lord to Zechariah, the son of Berechiah, the son of Iddo the prophet, saying, the Lord has been sore displeased with your fathers. Therefore say unto them, thus says the Lord of hosts: Turn unto Me, says the Lord of hosts, and I will turn unto you, says the Lord of hosts."*

It is important to date this prophecy correctly. It was through the military genius of this man Darius the Mede that mighty Babylon fell on the night of Belshazzar's feast. At that point the empire of Babylon fell and the empire of the Medes and Persians was fully established as their successor. We have a vivid account of that fateful night in the fifth chapter of Daniel. It was on that occasion that the hand wrote upon the plaster of the wall; and Daniel, an old man at that point, was called in to decipher the writing.

As Zechariah began his prophecy, this new empire had begun its consolidated rule over the civilized world. The bloody wars of expansion were, for the most part, ended, and then the enforced peace of a new empire had begun. Thus, we find that in verse 8 the *red horses* of warfare were standing still among the myrtle trees, their recent mission of devastation having just ended.

Zechariah 1:8-11: *"I saw by night, and behold a man riding upon a red horse, and he stood among the myrtle trees that were in the bottom; and behind him were red horses, speckled, and white. Then said I, O my lord, what are these? And the angel that talked with me said unto me, I will show you what these are. And the man that stood among the myrtle trees answered and said, 'These are they whom the Lord has sent to walk to and fro through the earth.' And they answered the angel of the Lord that stood among the myrtle trees, and said, 'We have walked to and fro through the earth, and, behold, all the earth sits still, and is at rest.'"*

Zechariah questioned the meaning of those things and received the reply given in verse 11. The earth was at rest for a while. This powerful peaceful rule of Persia lasted for over a hundred years. But even that lull in the world's conflicts was to have its end.

The Persians were generally gracious toward Israel. When they came to power they gave permission for the thousands of Hebrew captives that they inherited from Babylonian rule to return home, thus ending the seventy-year captivity. Ezra and Nehemiah give the account of this happening. But even after this, Israel was still under subjection to another nation, so in verse 12, we hear Zechariah crying out to the Lord for mercy and information about how long this state of affairs would go on.

Zechariah 1:12-15: *"Then the angel of the Lord answered and said, O Lord of hosts, how long will You not have mercy on Jerusalem and on the cities of Judah, against which You have had indignation these threescore and ten years? And the Lord answered the angel that talked with me with good words and comfortable words. So the angel that communed with me said unto me, Cry, saying, thus says the Lord of hosts: I am jealous for Jerusalem and for Zion with a great jealousy. And I am very sore displeased with the heathen that are at ease: for I was but a little displeased, and they helped forward the affliction."*

In verse 15, the Lord gave his answer. Although he had himself raised up these great empires to punish Israel and other nations that had been so wicked, the empires themselves proved to be no better, and each of them would have its own taste of defeat and humiliation in time. Even Persia, the world power that was then at ease, would come under judgment and destruction. So the horses that Zechariah first saw were at rest for a while between these periods of judgment. God, however, showed Zechariah another time not far into the future when these horses would again be sent out on their appointed missions. This new vision appears in Zechariah chapter 6.

HORSES AT WORK

Zechariah 6:1-8: *"And I turned, and lifted up my eyes, and looked, and, behold, there came four chariots out from between two mountains; and the mountains were mountains of brass. In the first chariot were red horses, and in the second chariot black horses; And in the third chariot white horses; and in the fourth chariot grisled and bay horses. Then I answered and said unto the angel that talked with me, 'What are these my lord?' And the angel answered and said unto me, 'These are the four spirits of the heavens, which go forth from standing before the Lord of all the earth. The black horses which are therein go forth into the north country; and the white go forth after them; and the grisled go forth toward the south country.' And the bay went forth, and sought to go that they might walk to and fro through the earth: and he said, 'Get you hence, walk to and fro through the earth.' So they walked to and fro through the earth. Then cried he upon me, and spoke unto me saying, Behold, these that go toward the north country have quieted my spirit in the north country."*

We have seen two views of these varicolored horses. The ones pictured in Revelation are simply horses on display. They are not connected with any particular events at all. The real purpose of this display is to introduce and explain the four great devices that God uses in the development of world events. The vision of the horses in the first chapter of Zechariah showed the horses at rest between missions. But now in chapter 6, we find them very much at work.

You will notice right away that the same four divisions are present. There are red, white, and black horses; and the last chariot is pulled by two varieties, grizzled and bay. This naturally seems to correspond with the two divisions concerning the fourth horse in Revelation that represents two devices of God, death and hell. So the grizzled and bay horses are death and hell as we shall see later.

Just as we dated the vision in chapter 1, we must be careful to date the fulfillment of this one also. In chapter 1, the empire was at rest, but now we see a prophetic view of the fall of this Persian Empire and the rise of the Greek Empire, which was the next one upon the world scene. This is the one that was represented by the belly and thighs of brass in Nebuchadnezzar's dream image. Now notice that these horses that Zechariah is watching come from between two mountains of brass. This agrees with the symbol of brass in Daniel 2 and represents the Greek Empire. But why are there two mountains? This empire had a short duration. It had only two rulers. It began under Philip of Macedonia and was finished by Alexander the Great, his son. And it immediately fell apart when Alexander died. Therefore, we can identify the time period of this vision as the age of the arrival of the Greek Empire.

There is more to the importance of this vision. From the beginning of history, the center of humanity had been in Asia, but the next step in God's plan was for that power center to be shifted from Asia to Europe. That was a high point in the development of human history. Zechariah was being permitted a glimpse into the near future when the last Asian empire would be defeated and replaced by the first European world empire.

Also of importance are the directions into which the various horses rode. The black ones were sent northward. Remember that the black horses represent God's blessings of national prosperity that are given on a conditional basis. The directions that are given in Bible prophecy are always in reference to the land of Israel, so these black horses rode northward from Israel. Israel is the Biblical center of the earth.

What is north from Israel? The land of Israel is bounded on the east by desert and on the west by the Mediterranean Sea. The travel routes into Israel enter either from the south or from the north. Although Babylon was almost due east of Israel, their invasion was described by Jeremiah as coming from the north (Jeremiah 1:15). But north was also the direction of the land routes into the Mediterranean "isles," or Europe as we know them today, and Europe is actually northwest of Israel. Therefore, north from Israel is a very general direction that takes in everything that is not south of Israel.

You will see on a map that Israel is on the western edge of the continent of Asia. So Zechariah's vision shows us the black horses of wealth and power moving from Asia to Europe, which is well north of Israel and Persia. This event actually carried the world balance of power from east to west as we observe the globe. A reference date for this event would be the year 331 BC when Alexander broke the yoke of the Persian Empire. This was about 190 years after Zechariah wrote these words. Here is more of God's prophecy fulfilled.

The black horses rode first as God laid a foundation of civilization in a new part of the world. And then the white horses were sent on the heels of the black ones. The white horses, as you will recall, represent the conquest of the Word of God. Therefore, God was foretelling that not long after the new European powers would arise, the Gospel of God's Son would be sent into their lands.

And so it was that when the Apostle Paul would have gone eastward into Asia (Acts 16:6-10), the Holy Spirit instead directed him westward into Macedonia, which was part of Greece. And westward the Gospel has gone ever since until it has, in recent centuries, approached Asia from the very opposite direction.

The Greek and Roman Empires were very important to the spread of the Gospel in this New Testament age. The relatively new system of Roman roads allowed Christians to travel far with the good news of salvation, and the Roman peace enforced the quietness that also made it possible.

Although there was a token reception of the Gospel south and east of Israel, you will see on modern maps of Europe and Asia that the "Christian" nations of the Old World lie in the directions into which the black and white horses rode, which was northward and then westward.

Now the south country into which the grizzled horses rode was the territory generally south of Israel. It included particularly Egypt, but Edom and even Babylon were not excluded from this. This was the area of the world from which the earliest conquering armies had marched.

The grizzled horses represent hell in a national sense. It is a removal from all that the black horses bring because they accompany the pale horse of death, which is like a negative image of the black. Egypt was a primary target for the grizzled horses of national death and disaster. The prophet Ezekiel, who lived not long before Zechariah, had this word to say on the matter of Egypt's decline and fall: "Thus says the Lord God; behold, I am against you, Pharaoh, king of Egypt, the great dragon that lies in the midst of his rivers, which has said, my river is my own, and I have made it for myself" (Ezekiel 29:3).

This scripture gives us the reason for God's judgment against Egypt. They had rejected a knowledge of the Creator God and had set themselves up as gods. In Paul's words, they were worshipping the creature more than the Creator. This same problem is blossoming again in our modern time as atheism gains more and more ground. The humanist proposition that states that there is no God is saying, in effect, that man is the highest intelligence in the universe, and thus man becomes his own idol. Shall people and nations that deny the existence of God be judged by the One whom they ignore? God said through Ezekiel that when he was through with Egypt, "all the inhabitants of Egypt shall know that I am the Lord" (29:6).

Here we see the balance of the Lord's justice in the hands of the rider upon the black horse tipping against Egypt. The black horses are leaving her borders for other fields, and the terrible grizzled horses enter in. Ezekiel was very descriptive in his prophecy against her as the Lord spoke, saying, "Behold I will bring a sword upon you, and cut off man and beast out of you. And the land of Egypt shall be desolate and waste" (29:8, 9). "It shall be the basest of all kingdoms; neither shall it exalt itself any more above the nations: for I will diminish them, and they shall no more rule over the nations" (29:15).

God was saying that Egypt would never again be the empire that it once was. It is almost needless to say that these words have been fulfilled to the letter. Babylon began the subjection of Egypt under Nebuchadnezzar. It has continued in various forms through the years, and now in our time, the Arabian stock is in control over the Egyptian remnant in their own land. Despite her rich heritage, Egypt remains a third-rate country.

And in Ezekiel's prophecy, there were other Southern countries that came under the influence of the Lord's grizzled horses at that time. In the thirtieth chapter, he speaks of the lands of Ethiopia, Libya, Lydia, and Chub; in Daniel 5, the empire of Babylon; and in Daniel 8, the empire of Persia. All these Southern lands came to the end of their world power as God judged them for refusing his knowledge and his ways. And as the grizzled horses entered, the black horses were removed far to the north of that part of the world.

Besides grizzled horses in the fourth chariot that Zechariah saw, there were also bay horses. This fourth chariot was unique in having two kinds of horses since the preceding three chariots had only one kind each. This corresponds to the fourth horse of Revelation 6 that also had a double identity, which was death and hell. So the bay horses of Zechariah's vision are the same as the pale horse that John saw, and they represent death.

In Zechariah's vision, these horses were sent to and fro through all the earth, and in this, the universality of death is seen. There is no man who can escape the blade of the rider upon the pale horse. However, the primary task of death, as seen in the Revelation account, is the accompanying of hell in his duties. And this is vividly seen in the activity of the grizzled horses of hell that were sent into the south country after the black horses of national power and prosperity were removed. These southern kingdoms came to be conquered one by one and suffered the tremendous loss of life that always accompanied defeat on the battlefield. Rampant disease, starvation, and even genocide were common to countries that were conquered in those days and, sometimes, in our own age as well.

At the beginning of chapter 6, Zechariah saw red horses along with the others, but he did not mention them again. As they came out from between the two mountains of brass that represented the new Greek Empire, they quickly did their work and were gone.

Accordingly, after Alexander the Great had established himself as absolute ruler of the earth, there followed an era of relative peace. The world had rest from the wars that had accompanied the building of four world empires within about three hundred years of time.

The Greek Empire with which Zechariah's vision began simply fell into smaller divisions through a lack of strong leadership after Alexander died. And then the Romans gradually established their influence, and there followed that period of enforced Roman "peace" that lasted approximately a thousand years. So we see how the red horses of war were finally held back from riding while the others carried on their duties. God had judged the Southern nations and then established sufficient peace on the earth so that the great change from the old to the new covenants could take place with the greatest possible efficiency.

CHAPTER 7

Issues at Stake and an Action Preview

In our study of historical end-time Bible prophecy, we have plunged into the Book of Revelation with an analysis of the seals that the Apostle John saw upon the great book of the future. The first four of these seals were symbolized by four horses of different colors. By comparing this Revelation passage to several Old Testament scriptures, we saw that these horses represent God's four great devices that he uses in accomplishing his work among the nations of the world.

Now after showing this vivid display of his techniques, our Lord next turns our attention to another one of the seals that introduce his book of prophetic mysteries of our age.

THE FIFTH SEAL

Revelation 6:9-11: *"And when he had opened the fifth seal, I saw under the altar the souls of them that were slain for the Word of God, and for the testimony which they held: And they cried with a loud voice, saying, How long, O Lord, holy and true, will You not judge and avenge our blood on those who dwell on the earth? And white robes were given unto every one of them; and it was said unto them, that they should rest yet for a little season, until their fellow servants also and their brethren, that should be killed as they were should be fulfilled."*

We have seen earlier that these seven seals are like the illustrated cover of a modern book that dramatically reveals something of the substance and issues that the book contains. This fifth seal is a statement of one of the *issues that are at stake in our world*. It is the question of how long it will be before God brings final triumph over the wicked. This coming time is spoken of in Acts 3:21 as the "times of restitution of all things."

Here at the beginning of this great prophecy of the New Testament age, we have this visionary appearance of many Old Testament saints, prophets, witnesses, and righteous people who had been killed because of their testimony of the truth of God. They surely include that number in Hebrews 11, the catalog of the faithful, of whom it is said that they endured mocking, torture, imprisonment, and stoning but *of whom the world was not worthy.*

The untimely deaths of these people rise to God as a question: "How long, O Lord?" This same issue has faced the world in every age, even our own. David often lamented in his psalms how evil appears to triumph over good in this life. The earth is a battleground between the prince of life and the prince of the power of the air, and this is part of the picture that appears on the "cover" of this book of the future events—"How long until restitution?"

It is not until the seals are all loosed and the book is opened, presenting the actual scenes of conflict, that the heavenly reply is given to this question. In chapter 13, verse 10, we read, "He that kills with the sword must be killed with the sword, Here is the patience and faith of the saints."

Christ shall indeed come again, and all things shall be put under his feet. All who belong to the devil "shall drink of the wine of the wrath of God," and "the smoke of their torment ascends up forever and ever. Here is the patience and faith of the saints" (Revelation 14:7, 11, and 12). So in this fifth seal, we see white robes of the righteousness of Christ given to these martyred saints as they rest until God's timetable is completed and the last righteous blood is shed on the earth.

THE SIXTH SEAL

Revelation 6:12-17: *"And I beheld when he had opened the sixth seal, and, lo, there was a great earthquake; and the sun became black as sackcloth of hair, and the moon became as blood; And the stars of heaven fell unto the earth, even as a fig tree casts her untimely figs, when she is shaken of a mighty wind. And the heaven departed. As a scroll when it is rolled together; and every mountain and island were moved out of their places. And the kings of the earth, and the great men, and the rich men, and the chief captains, and the mighty men, and every bondsman, and every free man, hid themselves in the dens and in the rocks of the mountains; And said to the mountains and rocks, Fall on us, and hide us from the face of him that sits on the throne, and from the wrath of the Lamb: for the great day of His wrath is come and who shall be able to stand?"*

Now we pass from the issues at stake to *the means by which they are achieved*. The sixth seal presents a display of earthly and heavenly phenomena that runs the gamut of the Bible's prophetic figurative language—the sun going black, the moon turning to blood, stars falling to the earth, and a geological upheaval so immense that no life could possibly exist afterward. It is needless to waste time considering whether these are real events that shall someday take place or not. The Bible itself gives us the answer if we will let it. They are not real happenings that shall supposedly come upon the world at some late day. They are prophetic symbols, as the Bible clearly shows.

For instance, the prophet Haggai warned of a time of great shaking that God would bring on the earth, saying, "I will shake the heavens, and the earth, and the sea, and the dry land; and I will shake all nations, and the desire of all nations shall come" (Haggai 2:67). This is a recognized prophecy of the first coming of Christ the Messiah and the events that would result from his entry into the world. This scripture is quoted in Hebrews 12:26 where it is explained that the shaking was the religious and social upheavals that accompanied the destruction of Israel as a nation and the beginning of the New Testament church.

God's "earthquakes" are like a sieve that separates the good from the bad in severe times of reckoning. Similarly, it is written in Malachi that Christ is like a refiner's fire and laundry soap (Malachi 3:2). He cleans and purges the earth. The prophet Joel spoke of a time when the sun would be turned into darkness and the moon into blood (Joel 2:31). That symbolic scripture is easily dated by going to the second chapter of Acts. Peter used this prophecy of Joel as his sermon text on the Day of Pentecost and applied it squarely to the events that were beginning to happen at that time. Paul also quoted from the same passage (Joel 2:32) in Romans 10, verse 13, and applied it to the same era that Peter did, which was the early days of the church. The sun that was turned into darkness was a figure of the ruling bodies of the Jewish nation. They were indeed wiped out when the Romans destroyed their nation in AD 70. The other symbols in this prophecy of Joel's can be likewise interpreted with a little comparative study and effort.

Another excellent example of this dramatic symbolic language is in Isaiah 13. That chapter contains Isaiah's prophetic announcement about the destruction of the Babylonian Empire that was soon to be accomplished by the up-and-coming Persians. The application of this chapter is very definite, and yet we have in verses 10 and 11 the same description of the sun and moon going dark. Verse 9 gives the motive for this tragedy, and it is to "destroy the sinners" out of the land. The sun and moon, of course, represented the various echelons of Babylonian authority. This was Babylon's "day of the Lord" (verse 6), which is a phrase that is used often in the Bible in regard to the Lord's severe periods of reckoning with nations.

The language of the sixth seal is very severe. In fact, the whole heaven is rolled up at one time like a window shade (6:14). This is fitting because this age of ours has contained some very dramatic days of reckoning at the hand of God. And the greatest will be at the time of the end when the authority of all nations will be taken away at the entrance of the King of kings. Sun, moon, stars, and all heavenly bodies representing people of all kinds and degrees will bow their knees at his coming.

So we see the sixth seal as a panoramic view of the intense action that would begin as soon as the trumpets should start their sounding. But there is yet one seal to be opened, and before it can be displayed, some other things must be set in order first.

We shall be seeing that the sounding of the first trumpet would herald the first great event in the Lord's itinerary for our age of time. That event was the transfer of the earthly kingdom of God from Jews to Gentiles. The job would be accomplished with earth-shaking tribulation for Israel, even the utter desolation of their nation and the dispersion of the Jews all over the world.

This destruction would be severe, but not total. If God had intended to wipe the slate entirely clean, there would be no need for chapter 7 of Revelation, but that was not his purpose. Back in Elijah's day, even in the midst of national apostasy, there were seven thousand Hebrews who were preserved from idolatry and its consequences. And Paul revealed in his time that God would repeat that accomplishment in the early days of the New Testament church. He said, "Even so then at this present time there is a remnant according to the election of grace" (Romans 11:5). Paul went on to say that this remnant was made up of the Jews of his own time who were inheriting the promises that had been symbolized in the covenant between God and Abraham. In other words, they were

Christians. How many Jews were there at that time who were saved to the early church? Perhaps the answer, either in accurate or symbolic count, is given here in chapter 7 of Revelation.

THE 144,000

Revelation 7:1-4: *"And after these things, I saw four angels standing on the four corners of the earth, holding the four winds of the earth, that the wind should not blow on the earth, nor on the sea, nor on any tree. And I saw another angel ascending from the east, having the seal of the living God: and he cried with a loud voice to the four angels, to whom it was given to hurt the earth and the sea, saying hurt not the earth, neither the sea, nor the trees, till we have sealed the servants of our God in their foreheads. And I heard the number of them which were sealed: and there were sealed a hundred and forty and four thousand of all the tribes of the children of Israel."*

Before the Lord would send out his destroying forces at the sounding of the first trumpet, there would have to be some provision made for the identification and protection of his servants. These were the Jewish Christians who constituted the church in its earliest years.

We Gentiles tend to forget that the early Christian church was 100 percent Jewish. In fact, it remained so for several years after Pentecost. As strange as it may seem, if a Gentile who was not a converted proselyte had presented himself for church membership during that time, he would not have been received. Only after Peter finally preached to Cornelius did that begin to change.

Chapter 7 begins with the four winds of the earth being held in check while the servants of God are sealed in their foreheads. These four winds have the same mission that the horses of the first four seals have, which is to initiate the events of change at the hand of God. It is not unusual for more than one symbol to be used for the same thing in the Bible. This occurs often in Christ's parables. These four devices of God are also represented as winds in Daniel 7 where they are used in the formulation of nations. Here, in chapter 7 of Revelation, their first mission would be destructive, as is seen in their power to hurt the earth and its contents.

So a certain number of the followers of God are sealed for identification so that they may escape the destruction that would be coming. There has been a huge amount of conjecture in Christian circles about who these

144,000 people are, and no doubt there have been many bad conclusions. But in this case, the Bible is still able to interpret itself if we let it.

In Revelation 14, we see the same throng described. This chapter is a brief specific prophecy about evangelism through our age. The first people to become the subjects of evangelism are these 144,000 people, and for this reason, they are called "the first fruits unto God and to the Lamb" (verse 4). We follow this description to James 1:18 where we read, "Of His own will begat He us with the word of truth, that we should be a kind of firstfruits of His creatures." So James identifies himself with a body of believers who are called first fruits. They are identified further in verse 1 where James addresses his letter to "the twelve tribes which are scattered abroad."

Therefore, we come full circle back to Revelation 7 where these 144,000 believers who are called the first fruits are also described by their divisions, and we find them to be of the twelve tribes of Israel. Here is the early Jewish church, sanctified, cleansed, and protected by the angels of God from the annihilation that the world was trying to bring upon them. All the tribes are listed in Revelation 7 but Dan. Were these twelve tribes still able to be identified in New Testament times? Actually, enough refugees filtered back to Israel from both the Assyrian and Babylonian captivities to continue tribal identities through the time of Christ although these records were not kept nearly as well as they had been in Old Testament times.

From the Day of Pentecost until Jerusalem was destroyed in AD 70 was about forty years. Considering the many thousands of believers that were converted in the early years of Acts, it is quite likely that Jewish converts would have reached at least 144,000 by the time their nation was destroyed. They were also added outside the confines of Judea in the many colonies of Rome into which the Gospel was spread.

This concept of sealing God's servants before destruction is not confined just to Revelation. Ezekiel had observed a similar event when he saw an angel passing through Jerusalem marking the foreheads of those who did "sigh and cry for the abominations that be done" in Jerusalem (Ezekiel 9:4). That occasion was the time of the conquest of Judah by Babylon. Obviously, the mark on the foreheads was not something that was visible to people. In Ezekiel's prophecy, it was put there for the observation of the destroying angels, and the same principle follows with the 144,000 marked ones in Revelation. One thing is certain, "The foundation of God stands sure, having this seal, the Lord knows them that are His" (II Timothy 2:19). And knowing them, he makes provision for them, "for He shall give His angels charge over you, to keep you in all your ways" (Psalm 91:11).

Revelation 7:9-17: *"After this I beheld, and, lo, a great multitude, which no man could number, of all nations, and kindreds, and people, and tongues, stood before the throne, and before the Lamb, clothed with white robes, and palms in their hands; And cried with a loud voice, saying, Salvation to our God who sits upon the throne, and unto the Lamb. And all the angels stood round about the throne, and about the elders and the four beasts, and fell before the throne on their faces, and worshipped God, Saying, Amen: Blessing, and glory, and wisdom, and thanksgiving, and honor, and power, and might, be unto our God for ever and ever. Amen. And one of the elders answered, saying unto me, What are these which are arrayed in white robes, and whence came they?' And said unto him, 'Sir, you know.' And he said to me, 'These are they which came out of great tribulation, and have washed their robes, and made them white in the blood of the Lamb. Therefore, are they before the throne of God, and serve him day and night in his temple, and he that sits on the throne shall dwell among them. They shall hunger no more, neither thirst any more; neither shall the sun light on them, nor any heat. For the Lamb which is in the midst of the throne shall feed them, and shall lead them unto living fountains of waters: and God shall wipe away all tears from their eyes.'"*

When we come to verse 9 of chapter 7, the scene changes. It begins with the words *after this*. This next multitude that John sees is far greater than the first, so much so that there would be no way for a person to number them. Instead of being from the tribes of Israel, they are from all nations, kindreds, peoples, and tongues. The white robes and the statement of praise identify them also as servants of the Lamb. Who are they? Here are the Gentile Christians of our age, far more numerous than the Jews and coming in at a later point in time.

They are described in verse 14 as coming out of great tribulation. This is historically accurate. Near the time when the Jews had come to their fullness in the church and the Gentile numbers were increasing fast, horrible persecutions began. The first major eruption began in Rome in AD 64 when Emperor Nero made the Christians the scapegoat for his heinous crime of burning the city of Rome. This began a long series of persecutions by the Romans against the church. Millions were killed. Then through the Middle Ages and especially during the Protestant Reformation, other millions have been added to the number.

The strange thing about persecution is that it also has a cleansing effect. The Christians who endured those events through the long centuries knew what dedication and sanctification were. The continuing verses describe them in their church devotions serving God in his temple (the church) and enjoying the many attributes and qualities of Christ their Redeemer.

So we see with John this vision of the church that was to come, each part in its proper order. Paul explained that the Gospel is the power of God unto salvation to everyone who believes, "to the Jew first, and also to the Greek" (Romans 1:16).

At this point in Revelation, all but one of the seven seals has been opened. The scene in chapter 7 has been set and the action is ready to begin. The varicolored horses are being held ready to be released, and there is a moment of silence before the earsplitting explosion of the first trumpet shall pierce the air. That trumpet would art the world down the track that God has prepared for this last age. But before that, there were some last-minute items to be set in order, therefore the pause.

CHAPTER 8

The Pause that Protects

Previously, we have seen that before God would begin to loose the eventful action of the first trumpet upon the earth, that important things would have to be set in order first. First, there would be the sealing of the early Jewish church from the awful destruction that only a few short years before had come upon their nation. The silence that is described in the verses below represents the absence of prophetic action. This is also seen in the holding back of the four horsemen in chapter 7, verse 1. Remember that they represent God's methods of accomplishing his will and purposes in the world as was seen in the first four seals.

THE SEVENTH SEAL

Revelation 8:1-6: *"And when he had opened the seventh seal, there was silence in heaven about the space of half an hour. And I saw the seven angels which stood before God, and to them were given seven trumpets. And another angel came and stood at the altar, having a golden censer; and there was given unto him much incense, that he should offer it with the prayers of all saints upon the golden altar which was before the throne. And the smoke of the incense, which came with the prayers of the saints, ascended up before God out of the angel's hand. And the angel took the censer, and filled it with fire of the altar, and cast it into the earth: and there were voices, and thunderings, and lightnings, and an earthquake. And the seven angels which had the seven trumpets prepared themselves to sound."*

This half hour of silence corresponds to the lull that resulted when the four winds were held back in chapter 7. God was not going to begin any new thing in world affairs while he was in the process of sealing his Hebrew servants and establishing the roots of his new church.

This same period of pause and preparation also appears in Daniel's prophecy. In fact, Daniel's vision concerning this period of time is so important and revealing that we will spend some time with it now.

THE SEVENTY-WEEK PROPHECY

In Daniel chapter 9, the Israelites were just finishing their seventy-year term of captivity in Babylon. They were surprised to have just learned from the prophet Jeremiah's writings that the time had arrived for them to be traveling home again to once again establish their nation and rebuild what had been destroyed.

According to the best Bible chronology, this was the year (on our calendar) 457 BC. They had been in forced bondage in Babylon and Persia for seventy years under God's orders because of their sins. And now God in prophecy to his servant Daniel makes a play on the number seventy, and he tells them that after the long seventy years is over, there will be another period of seventy—this time of weeks—and that after seventy weeks of time, certain other things would also be accomplished. They are all described in verse 24.

> *Seventy weeks are determined upon your people and upon your holy city to finish the transgression, and to make an end of sins, and to make reconciliation for iniquity, and to bring in everlasting righteousness, and to seal up the vision and prophecy, and to anoint the Most Holy.*

This is one of the most power-packed verses in all of the Bible. It speaks about the coming of the Lord Jesus Christ and his work of redemption and reconciliation upon the cross. And Gabriel said to Daniel that it would all come to pass within seventy weeks from the time that the King of Persia gave his command for Israel to return home. This was a very exact statement from the Lord and from Gabriel. It began a prophetic countdown of years.

Daniel 9:25: *"Know therefore and understand that from the going forth of the commandment to restore and to build Jerusalem unto the Messiah the prince shall be seven weeks, and three score and two weeks. The street will be built again and the wall, even in troublous times."*

Now 70 weeks is not a very long time, only about a year and a half. The angel gives the starting point of this 70-week period as the year when the imperial decree would go out to allow the Jews to go home (verse 25). This important date was the year 457 BC, a very notable year in Israel's history. Therefore, these 70 weeks, if they were weeks, would have ended within two years after that time, and all that the angel foretold would have happened by that time. However, they did not happen then. They did not happen until several centuries later when Christ came.

This problem brings us to one of God's prophetic measuring rules that he uses in his Word. In Ezekiel 14:4-6, we find the Lord instructing his prophet to lie upon his side for a certain number of days. These days, he was told, really represented years. And on another occasion, the Lord did the reverse and substituted years with days.

In Numbers 14:34, the forty days that Israel spied out the land of Canaan were changed into forty years, which were the length of time that they were delayed from entering the Promised Land. This *day for a year* principle carries over into the prophecies of Daniel and Revelation.

But why should the Bible sometimes use days to represent years? It is a kind of code that God used to represent the passage of time, and it was used for the same reason that other symbols were used throughout Bible prophecy. Furthermore, Christ Jesus used codes and symbols for the same reason when he taught through the parables. And his reason for doing that was so that unspiritual people should not understand the meaning of his messages (see Matthew 13:10-16).

We see, then, that the things that Gabriel told to Daniel did not take place within 70 actual weeks. Therefore, what do the 70 weeks mean? The 70 weeks contain 490 days (70 times 7). So the time span of this prophecy is really 490 years instead of 490 days. All that the angel foretold would take place within that time.

But next, in verse 25 of Daniel 9, we are given more specific information about the last seven years of this prophecy, years during which the important action would be taking place. As we have already seen, the starting date for this entire prophecy was the year 457 BC, when King Cyrus of Persia issued his decree for Israel to return to their homeland. Also in this verse is the date when the action that would fulfill the prophecy should begin so that all the purposes that are listed in verse 24 would be carried to completion. That year would be 69 weeks

(7 and three-score and 2) after 457 BC. Converting our days into years again, we find that it would be 483 years (69 times 7) after 457 BC.

We, of course, represent time before the birth of Christ with the letters *BC* and the time after his birth with *AD*. The monks who started this dating system lived during the Middle Ages, several hundred years after Christ. They calculated back to the time when Christ was thought to have been born, but as nearly as we can tell today, they missed the actual year by four or five years. Our Lord's birth probably occurred about the year 4 BC.

It is recorded in Luke 3:22-23 that Christ was about thirty years old when he began his ministry. So we see that from 4 BC, when he was born, until AD 26 was thirty years. Therefore, the 483-year period (or 69 "weeks") ends on exactly the date when the Son of God (the Most Holy One of verse 24) was revealed to the world. For research on his anointing, see Acts 10:38 and Luke 3:22. This is a truly amazing fulfillment of Bible prophecy.

But at this point, we are still left with seven years unexplained. They amount to the difference between the 69 weeks (483 years) of verse 25 and the 70 weeks (490 years) of verse 24. What would happen during that seven-year period?

In verse 27, it was said that Christ (the Messiah) would "confirm the covenant with many" for that "week" of seven years. This covenant was the covenant of the law that God gave through Moses, which Israel had broken over and over again. It was God's law, and it needed to be confirmed. Jesus did this confirming during his ministry to the Jewish nation, particularly in his Sermon on the Mount in the book of Matthew. A short time later, the revelation of the covenant of grace would be made by the New Testament apostles. But without the strictness of the old law, there can be no covenant of grace. Beginning at the start of his ministry, the Lord Jesus confirmed this covenant of God's law the three and one-half years before he went to the cross. Then he was crucified. This three and one-half years carries our calculations halfway through the last seven-year period of this prophecy and to the exact middle of the last "week." So at the exact center of that seven-year period, our Lord was crucified. When that happened, God ceased to recognize any more animal sacrifices as being acceptable (Hebrews 10:4). His own Son had become the ultimate sacrifice for sin. Therefore, in the angel Gabriel's words (verse 27), God caused these things to cease.

Although God did stop recognizing the animal sacrifices at the time of our Lord's death, the Jews continued to offer them for about forty years longer. Then in the year AD 70, God forcibly stopped them by having the temple in Jerusalem destroyed by the Romans. That was the "abomination of desolation" that is also described in verse 27. The heathen Roman army entering into Jerusalem and the holy temple was that abomination, and they brought great desolation to the city and region that have lasted even until our modern times.

Our calculations have now covered the period from 457 BC to AD 26 and then on for another three and one-half years to AD 29 or 30. There are now only three and one-half years remaining in the prophecy before the full 490 years would be spent. Remember that the angel said that the last "week" of seven years would be given to confirming the covenant to "many." Remember that Jesus Christ ministered only to the people of Israel and ordered his disciples not to go to the Gentiles. The covenant of both the law and grace would be later preached to the whole world, but for these last seven years of this remarkable prophecy, it would go only to the Jews. We saw how the Lord Jesus did this himself for one half of that period and then returned to heaven. For the last remaining three and one-half years the apostles and Christian witnesses confirmed the covenant of the law still only to Jews to finally fulfill all this prophecy. In fact, the early New Testament church was one hundred percent Jewish. But soon God began to change that. First, the Apostle Peter began to have dealings with Gentiles (Acts 14:46), and the church soon became more Gentile than Jewish in national make up.

So the Jewish nation was apparently the "many" to whom the covenant was confirmed. We have already seen them pictured in Revelation 7 as the sealed throng of 144,000. The first presentation of the Gospel of Christ to Gentiles must have come three and one-half years after the Crucifixion, or seven years after Christ's baptism, to completely fulfill the 70-week prophecy of Daniel.

Now let us tie together the seventieth week of Daniel's vision with the half hour of John's vision of Revelation 8:1. The old Hebrew calendar was different in some ways from our own. It contained twelve months of 28 days each, giving them a normal year of 336 days. This meant, of course, that they came up shorter at the end of the year than we do today. They handled this by adding an additional month to their calendar on their leap year, instead of one day, as we do. But their ordinary year contained only 48 weeks, divided equally into 12 months.

One week, therefore, was the *forty-eighth part* of the Hebrew year on their calendar. Also, one-half hour is the *forty-eighth part* of a twenty-four-hour day. So the one week of Daniel 9 is the forty-eighth part of a year while the half hour of Revelation 8 is the forty-eighth part of a day.

We have previously seen that in prophetic code, days and years are sometimes interchanged, and this is another example of it here. They both represent the same period, which was the three-and-one-half-year period of Christ's ministry and the three and one-half years that followed his ascension. This was the period during which God's covenant was confirmed to Israel only, before the Gentiles were brought into the kingdom of God and the nation of Israel was cut off (Matthew 21:48). Silence prevailed during that time. God would do no new thing among the nations while he was confirming his covenant with his people. He neither blessed nor punished anyone with his four great horsemen until the time of silence was up, and then the stillness was shattered as those horses burst as it were from the starting gate with the horrible devastation that accompanied the blowing of the first trumpet. So we have the statement in Revelation 8:2 that the angels with the trumpets are standing ready.

The scene that accompanies the opening of the seventh seal is a view of the most tender feeling between the two principal characters of the sealed book. See Revelation 8:3-4 above. They are the Lord Jesus Christ and his bride, the church. These saints whose prayers ascend up from the golden altar are caught as it were in a candid shot at their moment of greatest intimacy with their Lord. The golden altar was the one upon which incense was burned in the temple. That altar was symbolic of the closet of prayer of which Christ spoke, when hearts are humbled and communication travels between earth and heaven. This scene reminds one of the paper jacket on one of the popular romance novels that shows the male and female characters together in an intimate moment of contemplation with each other.

The golden altar of incense in the tabernacle and the temple was positioned in the holy chamber at the closest possible point to the mercy seat, actually against the curtain which separated the two rooms they occupied (Exodus 30:6). And that is what true prayer is like. It is the closest point to our Lord that we can reach in this room of life.

This scene is also one of God's savoring the fragrance of these prayers. Apparently, this offering of incense by the angel came at the end of the half hour of silence. Now considering what we have seen about the time frame of these events, this offering must have occurred in proper sequence. It occurred at the time of the end of the exclusive Gospel testimony to Israel, when the Word was about to be preached to Gentiles. The first account we have of this is in Acts 10:4, where Peter went under divine instruction to the house of Cornelius the Gentile. It was there that he made the statement, "Your prayers and alms are come up for a memorial before God." And along with Cornelius and his household there soon came a great host of Gentiles into the church, who hungered and thirsted for the true God of heaven.

The incense speaks not only of prayer but also of the righteous attributes of the people of God. In Cornelius's case, they were described as alms. It is the savor that makes God's children fragrant and flavorful, as Christ said, the salt of the earth. The great potential for good within the Gentile nations was about to be released in the world, a potential that had been shut up for thousands of years. It was not man's potential, of course, because he does not have any of himself, but as Paul said, "It is God which works within you," and God was about to do a great work.

Solomon had described the elect body of Christ as a garden of spices and fragrant plants: "A garden enclosed is my sister, my spouse; a spring shut up, a fountain sealed" (Songs 4:12). Then verse 16 seems to speak of that age of change and turmoil that saw the establishment of the New Testament Church: "Awake, O north wind; and come, you south; blow upon my garden, that the spices thereof may flow out." Then the church speaks back to Christ in reply: "Let my beloved come into His garden, and eat His pleasant fruits."

Therefore, the releasing of spiritual fragrance and flavor was a characteristic of that season in time when the New Testament church had its beginning. The seventh seal shows how this symbolic incense ascended to God as the final touch in setting the stage for the action that would be contained in the sounding of the seven trumpets.

We have now seen all seven of the seals removed from off the Book of the Revelation of our age. The issues and methods have all been made perfectly clear in the prophetic account so that there should be no misunderstanding about the cause and purpose of God's work in our day. It is a work of the wonderful revelation of his severe justice and everlasting mercy upon a world of already redeemed saints that had been "tossed with tempest and not comforted" (Isaiah 54:11-13).

Darkness had covered the earth for the four thousand years since Adam and Eve had fallen and plunged man into sin, but then our Lord spoke to his great universal church and said, "The Lord shall arise upon you, and His glory shall be seen upon you, and the Gentiles shall come to your light, and kings to the brightness of your rising" (Isaiah 60:2-3).

CHAPTER 9
The Trumpets of Change

The violence that has been done to the Book of Revelation by well-meaning scholars and interpreters in our time is absolutely amazing. They have flung the book here and there in every direction through time, bringing forth horrendous explanations that would rock the very universe if they ever actually happened.

And all the while, the real and lucid explanations of the Apostle John's fantastic revelations were right there under their very noses in our history books—which no one seems to want to read anymore.

The Apostle John made the statement at the beginning of his Revelation that God was showing things to him that *must shortly come to pass*. This is a vastly important statement. The future events that John saw and wrote about have been already happening at their various appointed times for almost two thousand years now. The Book of Revelation is all about the journey of the people of God—the Church of Jesus Christ—through this last age of time and the warfare in which she would be engaged. It ends with the glorious view of the new age that will be coming after this one and the final judgment of the wicked and restitution of all things.

And what is the purpose of all this? It is significant what the Lord Jesus told his disciples shortly before his Crucifixion, "And now I have told you before it is come to pass, that, when it is come to pass, you might believe." But if one does not see the fulfillment of most of Revelation revealed through the past several hundred years of history, then he has no choice but to apply it all to a time which is yet to come. Ignorance of world history is a tragic fault, especially in the proper interpretation of the Bible's prophecies.

In John's vision, there were seven trumpets blown, meaning that there would be seven outstanding events that would happen during this last age of time—which is that span of time that would last from John's day until the time when the Lord comes back. At our present point in time, six of those events have already happened, standing out clearly in history, and only one more is yet to come.

UNFINISHED BUSINESS

It seems that John the Baptist had made an announcement about an ax being laid to the root of some trees (Matthew 3:10). Those trees were still standing when Christ's earthly ministry ended. They represented the Hebrew people who, at one time, had been *trees of righteousness, the planting of the Lord* (Isaiah 61:3), but—through stubbornness, rebellion, and pride—had become like the barren fig tree that the Lord had cursed and had withered away from its roots (Matthew 21:19).

It is certain that the root, which is Christ, was left intact and that the new Gentile branches would be grafted onto it in due time; but the withered top must first be hewn away by that fearful ax that God wields upon the disobedient.

Thus, it must be that a tree would have to fall in the forest of the nations of men, but as in all things that God does, much good would come out of it. Paul testified to this truth when he wrote that "through their fall salvation is come to the Gentiles" (Romans 11:11). Also, the Lord Jesus made plain what would be happening when he told some of his contemporaries, "The kingdom of God shall be taken from you and given to a nation bringing forth the fruits thereof" (Matthew 21:43).

Since God saw fit to prune off the Israelites and graft in the Gentiles, we of the Gentiles might be tempted to assume that we are made of better stuff that they were. But that is not so. The Hebrews were only typical of all humanity, and that is no doubt why God chose them in the first place—to show to all the world just what mankind is really like. Paul wrote to the Roman Gentile Christians, "Well, because of unbelief they were broken off, and you stand by faith. Be not highminded, but fear. For if God spared not the natural branches, take heed lest He spare not you" (Romans 11:20-21). Obviously, New Testament Christians are by nature different from Old Testament Jews. They were of a natural blood line, but we are of a spiritual line, born of God and sanctified of his Spirit. That makes all the difference for all Christians and sons of God, whether they are nationally Gentiles or nationally Jews.

So we see John the Baptist foretelling the destruction of the tree of Israel. But when did it actually fall? We know that the Lord Jesus was a Jew after the flesh who preached and ministered almost exclusively to Jews. Also, the priesthood of Aaron was still in authority and power at that time. Jesus recognized that when he said, "The scribes and Pharisees sit in Moses' seat. All things therefore whatsoever they bid you, observe and do, but do not after their works, for they say and do not" (Matthew 23:2-3).

THE LAST STROKE

When did that authority that the Jews had come to its end? When was the Jewish trunk finally cut off and the Gentile branches grafted in? The final strokes began when our Savior died. As his flesh was torn and pierced, God, by his invisible hand, reached down and ripped into two pieces the glorious veil that was hanging in the beautiful temple that Herod had just newly rebuilt. He was finished with that veil forever because the separation between God and sinful man was being abolished through the death of his Son. Therefore, we read in the Book of Hebrews that Christ, when he died, entered the holiest place of God. "By a new and living way, which He has consecrated for us through the veil, that is to say, His flesh" (Hebrews 10:20).

Things happened quickly after that. The church on the Day of Pentecost was completely Jewish, of course, but it did not stay that way. The apostles were sent out, and Peter first and then Paul began their witnessing to Gentiles, and they started coming to Christ in vast numbers while the Jewish converts began to dwindle away.

The very reality of the eternal kingdom of God began coming to light as the ancient types and shadows drifted away. And drifting away along with the shadows were the children of Israel "who serve under the example and shadow of heavenly things" (Hebrews 8:5).

The final stroke of the ax in this operation occurred in the year AD 70. At that time, a Roman army under the general Titus surrounded and laid siege to the city of Jerusalem. After five months, they had battered down her walls and laid the city waste. We are told by the Jewish historian, Josephus, that over a million Jews lost their lives in that conflict, and ninety-five thousand were taken captive. History plainly records the horrors of viciousness, murder, and even cannibalism that took place in Jerusalem during those days. So the Lord spoke truly of that time when he said, "For then shall be great tribulation, such as was not since the beginning of the world to this time, no nor ever shall be" (Matthew 24:21).

BLOOD, FIRE, AND HAIL

There are two sides and two messages that belong to the wonderful event of birth of our Savior into the world. This dual meaning can readily be seen in one of the important prophecies about the event, recorded in Isaiah 61:2. There it tells us that this Savior who was coming would bind up the brokenhearted and open prison doors to those who were bound. But it also says that he would "proclaim the acceptable year of our Lord, and the day of vengeance of our God." What is this saying to us? Just that Christ would not only be bringing salvation, but some terrible destruction as well.

This duality is apparent also in the prophecy of Malachi. In chapter 3, verse 2, we are advised, "But who may abide the day of His coming, for He is like a refiner's fire." And so he was. In chapter 23 of Matthew, he pronounced woe and destruction no fewer than seven times upon the generation of that day. Unless we should think that the Lord Jesus was unreasonably hard on the Jewish people to whom he preached, let's remember that he found and judged them to be more unrepentant than Tyre and Sidon and more degenerate than the city of Sodom. These hard cold facts are clearly recorded in Matthew 11.

So it should not be surprising that he would pronounce a judgment upon them that was unique and thorough. He also said to them, "That upon you may come all the righteous blood shed upon the earth from the blood of righteous Abel unto the blood of Zacharias, whom you slew between the temple and the altar. Verily I say unto you, all these things shall come upon this generation" (Matthew 23:35-36). Therefore, the first major event that happened in God's agenda for this last age of ours was the casting away of the nation of Israel from participation in the kingdom of God here on this earth.

Paul makes the point in Romans 1:15 that it was truly a "casting away." But he also points out in the same chapter of Romans that it was not a total wipeout. There was then, and still is today, a remnant of Jewish people who believe the Gospel of Christ and who function in the New Testament kingdom. But the nation as a whole lost it and, by the hand of God, have been dispersed out of their homeland into the nations of the earth as strangers and pilgrims. Only now in our generation has the tide turned, and some of Israel is finally returning to their possession and inheritance.

THE FIRST TRUMPET

Here is the language of the first trumpet—the first major event to mark the beginning of this final age of time:

> *And the angel which had the seven trumpets prepared themselves to sound. The first angel sounded, and there followed hail and fire mingled with blood, and they were cast upon the earth. And the third part of the trees were burnt up, and all green grass was burnt up.* (Revelation 8:6-7)

This is God's symbolic, prophetic description of the removal of Israel from the earthly kingdom of God. Each word has prophetic meaning, as we shall see. First, the hail and fire were literal enough although it was not hail as we think of it. The symbolic importance of hail here is that it comes suddenly, crushes the land, and leaves destruction after it.

Letting the Bible be its own interpreter, we can go to the Books of Job and Isaiah for the explanation about God's hail. In Job 38:22-23, there is this interesting statement about God's special hail: "Have you seen the treasures of the hail, which I have reserved against the time of trouble and against the day of battle and war?" This is strange hail, is it not, that it should be used in God's warfare. As early as 675 BC, the prophet Isaiah had seen the progressive corruption of Israel and had been moved to prophecy, "Behold, the Lord has a mighty and strong one, which as a tempest of hail . . . shall cast down to the earth with the hand" (Isaiah 28:2).

And then in verse 17, he described the effect the hail would be having and its reason for coming: "Judgment also will I lay to the line, and righteousness to the plummet. And the hail shall sweep away the *refuge of lies.*" So there it is—a *mighty and strong army* that would be coming at God's command to obliterate a nation that had become a refuge of lies.

Can we assume that this could apply to the Israel of Christ's time? Well, in John 8:44, on another of those occasions when he was confronting the religious authorities of the Jews, he said, "You are of your father the devil, and the lusts of your father you will do. When he speaks a lie he speaks of his own, for he is a liar and the father of it."

So the lies were there. Now what about the refuge of lies? The Jews of Christ's time apparently thought they were safe. Isaiah 28:15 tells us that they had made a "covenant with death." This was apparently the agreement their leaders had made with the Roman occupation force whereby they thought they would continue to have peace between them. They even boasted to Pilate when he was examining Jesus that they recognized no king but Caesar. But in their hearts, they had a different attitude, and this was just another one of their lies.

This peace agreement broke down forty years later when the Jews rebelled against the power of Rome. At that time, Isaiah's prophecy was fulfilled (28:15-18) when the land that was a refuge of lies experienced an overflowing scourge passing over it. That was in AD 70 when the Romans destroyed their city. The hail did its work very well.

Next, we notice in the language of the first trumpet that along with the hail came fire mingled with blood. Since we have previously noticed the comparison of Israel a tree that was about to be hewn down, it would be proper here to see the destination of those trees. Jesus said, "Every tree that brings not forth good fruit is hewn down and cast into the fire" (Luke 3:9). There are two important things that should be observed here. First, there is an indication that there would be a selection made between trees according to their fruit. Some would be cut down and others would be left standing. Therefore, we have the expression in Revelation 8:7 that the third part of the trees were burned up. How does this apply to Israel of that time? Well, the sect of the Pharisees numbered only about six or seven thousand, and of that number, many were good men, and some even believed on Christ secretly. So of the Pharisees and the other corrupt religious sects, all the individuals who were subject to God's hottest wrath, were probably in the minority among the people and were quite possibly a third of the teachers and leaders of that day.

But they were indeed trees—which is to say that they were men of influence and stature who stood above the lesser shrubs in the forest of men. And they had influence. On the night of Christ's arrest, they moved among the people and prompted them to call for his death.

INTO THE FIRE

The other important point about this is that the trees were cast into the fire. Simply speaking, fire represents the wrath of God in judgment. There is an everlasting lake of it reserved as the eternal abode of the devil, his angels, and his children (Revelation 20:15). In the Old Testament, God poured fire and brimstone on the cities of Sodom and Gomorrah.

But fire is also used figuratively in the Bible. As the Old Testament ended, Malachi foresaw the coming of Christ and the destruction that would be coming upon Israel. He wrote, "For behold, the day comes which shall burn as an oven, and all the proud, yes, and all who do wickedly shall be stubble. And the day that comes shall burn them up, says the Lord of Hosts, and it shall leave them neither root nor branch" (Malachi 4:1).

Prophetically, the root that Malachi mentioned must be the revealed Christ in the kingdom of God. Isaiah called him a *root out of dry ground* (Isaiah 53:1). The branch seems to indicate their own removal as a nation from the New Testament kingdom. So into the fire the nation went.

But that was not all. The first trumpet also tells us that the fire and hail were mingled with blood. We can see that this was the nature of the judgment they received. It was a bloody event, and there were the horrors of violent death all around when their city suffered and fell.

Another important part of the first trumpet's message was that all green grass was burnt up. We can figure by now that the grass must represent some portion of the people who were destroyed in the siege of the city. Obviously, the grass would be different from the trees, not only in stature but also in number. And all the grass was burnt up. Apparently, whereas the trees were leaders of the people, the grass must designate the more common people, whose only outstanding characteristic was their hearts of rebellion against God, his Word, and his messengers.

This seems to be the same thing that we see in Psalm 37:1-2. There it says, "Fret not yourself because of evildoers, neither be envious against the workers of iniquity. For they shall soon be cut down like the grass."

Wherever Christ went and ministered among the people, he found believers and unbelievers. When he entered Jerusalem for the last time, the people welcomed him as a king. A few days later, some of those same people were in the streets calling for his blood, and they said, "His blood be on us and on our children." God obliged them. Forty years later, the destruction came, and that portion of the common people who cared nothing for their Messiah felt the fire of the wrath of God.

Not all the leaders or common people in Jerusalem were destroyed in the siege of Jerusalem. Christ's prophetic warning to believers is in Luke 21:20-22. There he warned about the coming destruction and told the believers that they should flee from the city when they saw it coming. History tells us that is exactly what took place. The Christians saw the Roman legions coming and fled to the rock fortress city of Pella, where they escaped from the war.

Chapter 10

The Second Trumpet

God does not want a vacuum in his kingdom on the earth. When the children of Israel were cast out, it was necessary in God's economy for the resulting void to be filled up, and this process was well under way even before Jerusalem was destroyed by the Romans.

Surely it was a heart-rending occasion for God's national heritage to become scattered abroad over all the earth with their eyes blinded to the truth of the revealed Messiah. And what of the promises he had made to them in past times? What of the glowing prospects he had sworn by the prophets of old would come to Zion—the prospects of national deliverance, prosperity and glory?

Well, those promises still belonged to Zion and would become finally fulfilled in a far more marvelous was than the Hebrew ancients had ever dreamed. But instead of belonging to that hill in Jerusalem called Zion, which became blood smeared by the Roman destroyers, these promises passed to another Zion, which a New Testament writer revealed as being the church of Jesus Christ. He wrote, "But you are come to Mount Zion, and unto the city of the living God, the heavenly Jerusalem, and to an innumerable company of angels, to the general assembly and *church of the firstborn.*"

This is one of the keys that is often overlooked by those who seek to interpret the prophets entirely in terms of a national Israel rather than a spiritual one—that Zion is indeed one of the prophetic code names for the church. Thus, the meaning of that plaintive cry from Isaiah's writing comes to us, "But Zion said, the Lord has forsaken me, and my God has forgotten me" (Isaiah 49:14).

Well, did he forsake Israel? We may be certain that he did forsake national Israel, but let us hear what the Lord replies to them: "The children which you shall have, after you have lost the other, shall say in your ears, the place is too small for me; give place to me that I may dwell" (20).

So then, after the loss of her first children, which were Jews outwardly, there would be coming in those who would be Jews spiritually, or inwardly, whom Paul described in Romans 2:29. It would be these who would expand Zion far beyond the confines of a mere natural nation and would fulfill to the last detail the promises of God contained in the prophecies of old.

A BURNING MOUNTAIN

It becomes plain to see at this point that the second greatest event of our age—after the casting away of Israel—was the establishment and growth of the kingdom of God within the church among the Gentiles. And this is what is proclaimed by the angel with the second trumpet:

> *And the second angel sounded, and as it were a great mountain burning with fire was cast into the sea; and the third part of the sea became blood; and the third part of the creatures which were in the sea and had life died; and the third part of the ships were destroyed.* (Revelation 8:8, 9)

We should not miss the expression *as it were* because we find that this was no more a mountain of actual stone and earth than was the Zion that Paul had said was the church. Actually, the Zion he had spoken of was Mount Zion, and here we find the church of Christ as Mount Zion being strangely cast into the sea.

Once again, this was not a literal sea either but a symbolic one which represented the sea of humanity that, like the watery sea, covers this earth of ours. This symbol is clearly enough taught in the scriptures. Two references that can be quickly given are the *peoples, multitudes, nations, and tongues* that are revealed as the *waters* in Revelation 17:15. Another is the *sea* of Daniel 7:2 that produced an array of kingdoms and governments from its depths.

The beautiful truth that God reveals to us in these two symbols of the mountain and the sea is of the New Testament church of Jesus Christ being given to the masses of the Gentiles by means of God-sent preachers being placed in their midst.

So Isaiah further declares, "How beautiful upon the mountain are the feet of him that brings good tidings . . . that publishes salvation" (Isaiah 52:7).

And those glad tidings included this promise, "You shall see and flow together, and your heart shall fear and be enlarged; because the abundance of the sea shall be converted unto you, the forces of the gentiles shall come unto you" (Isaiah 60:5). So the mountain was cast into the sea with all the force and abrupt "splash" that accompanied the spiritual display on the Day of Pentecost when the church age began. About three thousand souls were added that first day.

Next, we see that the mountain was on fire. It would be too simple to merely say that the church should be on fire for God. Something of a deeper meaning is seen in Zechariah's expression concerning the new Gospel age: "And I [God] will bring the third part through the fire, and will refine them as silver is refined, and will try them as gold is tried: they shall call on my name, and I will hear them: I will say, it is my people: and they shall say, the Lord is my God" (Zechariah 13:9).

So this fire is for refining the children of God while they seek to live lives of righteous obedience to him as the Gospel and the church lead them into denying themselves and the world and following their Lord Christ. You may recall that in Malachi 3:2, he is revealed as a "refiner's fire" who shall "sit as a refiner and purifier of silver."

Perhaps you have found yourself, from time to time, in God's efficient blast furnace, as it were. If God loves you, you have been there, "for whom the Lord loves He chastens, and scourges every son whom He receives" (Hebrews 12:6). It is then that our works are examined by the master builder who sees and knows all about us and consumes our misdeeds in the furnace of his love and wrath, for "every man's work shall be made manifest; for the day shall declare it, because it shall be revealed by fire: and the fire shall try every man's work of what sort it is" (I Corinthians 3:13).

The end result of this burning process is a mountain of humble saints whose only claim is that statement made by Zechariah (above), "The Lord is my God." How precious is that gold, and how beautiful are the feet! For his ministers also are made *a flame of fire* (Hebrews 1:7).

In Zechariah's statement about the fire, the point is made that a third part would pass through it. This one-third is also mentioned three times in the scripture of the second trumpet that we are examining, so something should be said of its meaning.

It should be thoroughly understood that the passing of the kingdom of God from the Jews to the Gentiles was a momentous event. It was a subject of prophecy for hundreds of years before it ever came to pass. It was first mentioned by Noah in his age-old prophecy to his three sons, Shem, Ham, and Japheth, when he said, "God shall enlarge Japheth, and he shall dwell in the tents of Shem; and Canaan shall be his servant" (Genesis 9:27).

THE THIRD PART

The Bible tells us in the Book of Genesis that the world's peoples are divided into three parts, which trace their ancestry to these three sons of Noah. This opens the door to a world of speculation and interpretation, of course, for which there is little space here—so the following comment will be brief. The Jews, being descended from Shem, lost the kingdom of God in its physical or national sense, and it passed from them to the sons of Japheth. These are the Gentiles, broadly speaking, which comprise the peoples of European stock that we know today—most Americans being included. Africans and Asians are generally understood to be descended from Ham and are not Gentiles in the proper prophetic sense of the word although the name is sometimes applied to them also. This does not mean that they are not included in the covenant of redemption, but it does mean that during most of the last two millenniums they have not been chosen by God to perpetuate the Gospel and the church in this particular age. Now, however, that is beginning to change as the Gospel is flooding Africa and Asia. The Japhethites have done that and are still doing it, just as Noah had prophesied some four thousand years ago. History bears this out.

Thus, the expression *one-third* takes in the descendants of Japheth who comprised the old Roman Empire and who also have made up the so-called Christian nations of recent times. We dwell in Shem's tent—those of us who are believers in Christ—which is the revealed kingdom of God in the earth or, to put it simply, the church. God has indeed enlarged us as Noah said he would. And Isaiah also picks up the theme, saying, "Enlarge the place of your tent . . . lengthen your cords and strengthen your stakes; for you shall break forth on the right hand and on the left; and your seed shall inherit the Gentiles" (Isaiah 54:2, 3). And so it has been.

Returning now to the words of the second trumpet, we observe that the third part of the sea became blood. This is a simple description of the further bloodshed that followed along with the establishment of the church.

Remember that Christ had said, "I come not to bring peace, but a sword." And that sword has been severely felt by the church, beginning with the beheading of John the Baptist.

The history of the first three hundred years of church history is a thoroughly bloody account of the attempt by the governments in power to obliterate Christ's followers. It was no surprise to them, however. The Lord Jesus had given them plenty of warning about what was to come, and many were his disciples who died joyfully that they were counted worthy to suffer with him.

And yet the Lord's followers multiplied. The overwhelming flood of truth and conviction that was stirred up by the sinking of that mountain into the sea swept into every crevice of the Roman Empire. And so Tertullian, a prominent disciple of that time, wrote, "We are of yesterday, yet we have filled your empire, your cities, your towns, your islands, your tribes, your camps, castles, palaces, assemblies, and senate."

Next, we consider the effect that this mountain had upon the sea of men. The passage above stated that the third part of the creatures, which were in the sea and had life, died. So this sea, like all seas, contained creatures that were not a part of the seawater itself (people) although they did live in it. In this symbolic case, they are creatures whose place is among people, and it is the people who give them life and being.

Considering what actually happened when this sea was disturbed, it is a short step over to Romans 1:23 and 25 where we find these creatures revealed as the idols of men that flourish in nations that do not have the truth of the Gospel of God. Without that truth, the Gentile peoples of old had followed the line of least resistance to the flesh and had, as Paul said, "changed the glory of the incorruptible God into an image made like to corruptible man, and to birds and four footed beasts, and creeping things and worshipped and served the *creature* more than the Creator." These false gods, then, were the creatures that died—a third of the world's supply of them, belonging to the Gentile sons of Japheth.

This also was a promise of prophecy concerning the Gospel day. God had said that "in that day I will cut off the names of the idols out of the land, and they shall be no more remembered" (Zechariah 13:2).

From the gods of the Druids of England to the fabulous deities of the Greeks, they all were toppled from their pedestals in the hearts and minds of men like the ridiculous fish-tailed statue of Dagon that had fallen on its face before the ark of the covenant of God (I Samuel 5:3). The eternal covenant revealed in the Gospel of Christ accomplished the same work as the ark had, but on a much grander scale.

SATAN'S NAVY

As it was with the creatures, so it was also with the ships: "And the third part of the ships were destroyed." The ships and shipping that is presented here is a marvelous symbol of the tradesmen of the earth who ply the waters of mankind, seeking profit as they can find it. They are exposed in the eighteenth chapter of Revelation as religious practitioners who trade with mystic Babylon—merchants who have been made rich by her (verse 15): *shipmasters, ships, and sailors.*

Among their wares that they buy and sell are the *souls of men* (verse 13). Further light is shed upon the subject by the Apostle Peter who identified them as those who bring in "damnable heresies." He explains, "And many shall follow their pernicious ways; by reason of whom the way of truth shall be evil spoken of. And through covetousness shall they with feigned words make merchandise of you" (II Peter 2:2, 3). Many are the children of God who have sold out to these deceivers lock, stock, and barrel.

These ships are the inventions and worldly philosophies of men and the devil that are built in the shipyards of good intentions and vain glory. They are devices that have been contrived to reconcile religions with the way of the flesh and clothe depraved sinners in cloaks of respectability.

These ships buy the natural lives (souls) of men by explaining away the horror of original sin and total depravity and offering instead a misplaced faith in the humanistic spirit of man. They include the rituals and sacrifices that are used to soothe consciences that have been pricked by the Holy Spirit of God. They include the God dishonoring theories of biblical "higher criticism," atheistic "science," and atheistic applications of psychology. They are all subtle and all seek to work within the framework of the church, but in the end, all of them equally deny the Lord's Christ.

A QUIET HABITATION

This sounds as if they are still here today, does it not? Well, they are indeed, but they are not in churches where the Spirit of God has free expression. Although they did have a strangle hold upon the temple worship of Christ's day, they have been cut off from true worshipers in our time.

As long as there are men and women around who try to elevate the flesh at the expense of God's glory there will be plenty of these ships at sea, but they cannot float in a church where the full Gospel is preached and believed.

Once more, Isaiah offers the master stroke of expression as he sees Mount Zion without these ships and in her full glory: "Look upon Zion, the city of our solemnities; your eyes shall see Jerusalem a quiet habitation, a tabernacle that shall not be taken down . . . But the Lord shall be unto us a place of broad rivers and streams, wherein shall go no *galley with oars, neither shall gallant ship* pass thereby" (Isaiah 33:20, 21).

How beautifully they present themselves, these gallant ships at sea, as under full sail they barter men's lives from port to port! But how much more beautiful are the feet of them that publish good tidings upon the mountain!

And Zion herself, the city of our solemnities, is "beautiful for situation, the joy of the whole earth" (Psalm 48:2).

Chapter 11

The Third and Fourth Trumpets

The history of the kingdom of God in this world is one of bright hopes, successes, and crashing disappointments. The Garden of Eden episode is perhaps the most vivid illustration of this truth. Then there were the sons of Noah going forth into a newly cleansed world with high anticipation that were given a severe setback at the Tower of Babel. Later, the glory of Israel under the early kings was ground into the earth under the heels of the Babylonians.

And then, after long centuries of such disappointments, the promised Messiah finally did come but only to inform his followers that he would be betrayed and killed. All this seems tragic for man but, nonetheless, fulfills God's plans and purposes. Such was the picture of the church of Jesus Christ as the New Testament age got under way. The commission had been given, and the world was waiting for the sunrise of new truth to burst upon it.

In the first three hundred years, great strides were made even in the face of the severest kind of persecution, including execution of believers by fire and wild beasts. By the fourth century, new congregations of Christians had spread all the way from Israel, across Europe to the North Sea, and perhaps, half the population of the Roman Empire had identified itself with the church in some way.

The cost had been dear, but the victory was full of promise. By this time, the Roman government had given up its endeavor to suppress the church, and the way seemed clear for a long era of peace under God's blessing.

But there was a foreboding shadow that fell across the peaceful scene. There had been repeated warnings by the New Testament writers about an even worse danger than governmental oppression, and it was fast approaching. And thus the time had come for the trumpet call from the third angel of John's Revelation.

THE THIRD TRUMPET

> *And the third angel sounded, and there fell a great star from heaven, burning as it were a lamp, and it fell upon the third part of the rivers, and upon the fountains of waters; and the name of the star is called Wormwood. And the third part of the waters became wormwood, and many men died of the waters because they had been made bitter.* (Revelation 8:9-10)

As we make our study of these trumpets and the events they symbolize, we should be careful to keep in mind that this is church business we are viewing. Some writers apply some of these symbols in Revelation to the invasion of the barbarian hordes that swept in against the Roman Empire and finally subdued it. These events were important, of course, but they had no effect upon the church except to, quite probably, hasten its spread across the continent.

These seven trumpets rather reveal the seven greatest events that pertain to the church in our age, and after the fruitful establishment of the church as revealed in the second trumpet, the next greatest event was her shameful descent into apostasy. The bride of Christ, like Mother Eve of old, fell to the seductive enticements of her archenemy, Satan, who had been waiting patiently in the wings for his moment of opportunity to come.

THE GREAT PRETENDER

As the third trumpet sounded, John saw a great star fall from heaven. When we think of the stars in scripture, there comes to mind the bright and morning star, which is Christ bringing his light into a dark world. And then he shines as the day star with his rays of truth during this Gospel day. However, there are other stars, even evil ones, whom Jude describes as "wandering stars, to whom is reserved the blackness of darkness forever" (Jude 13). This would be a fitting judgment for an evil star, that it should be darkened forever.

The star that fell was burning as it were a lamp. The expression *as it were* tells us that it was an imitation of a lamp, very similar in some ways, but far from being the genuine article. The Psalmist David said that the Word of God was as a lamp unto his feet, and we have seen that lamp as it brightened men's hearts and minds in the old Roman world.

But the time came when the church grew to become so influential and powerful that it started to be popular with the wrong kind of people. Anything of value can have a cheap imitation made of it, and frequently that happens. Therefore, we have here the entrance of God's cheap imitation, who is Satan, the great pretender.

Satan has always wanted to be like God. Isaiah said this about him, "For you have said in your heart, I will ascend into heaven, I will exalt my throne above the stars of God. I will be like the Most High" (Isaiah 14:13-14). And this was exactly the temptation that Satan used against Eve in the garden—that she and Adam would be as gods if they would eat of the forbidden fruit. He also used it against man and his civilization at the Tower of Babel, tempting them to build a tower that would reach up to heaven. Satan longs to be like God.

And so we see Satan after he had fought against the church with every weapon he could muster, finally giving up the fight and assuming the new attitude that if you can't beat them, then join them. And join them he did.

During the reign of the emperor Theodosius in the fourth century, church membership was actually made compulsory by the Roman government. Can you imagine the result? Unrepentant, unbelieving people began pouring into the churches, and quickly made their way into positions of leadership. Thus, the light of the lamp of the Word of God began to be adulterated with all the vain philosophies of men and devils.

The Apostle Paul had by inspiration warned about this in his letters. He said, "For such are false prophets, deceitful workers, transforming themselves into the apostles of Christ. Therefore, it is no great thing if his ministers also be transformed as the ministers of righteousness, whose end shall be according to their works" (II Corinthians 11:13-15).

Also, when writing to another church about the second coming of Christ, he wrote, "For that day shall not come except there come a falling away first" (II Thessalonians 2:3).

Like the flash of a falling star, these false prophets and deceitful workers ascended the high places of the churches, burning like a lamp with teaching that sounded good but were absolutely contrary to real Bible truth. The church of Jesus Christ had succeeded in conquering the Roman Empire by changing its religion. But then the empire turned and conquered the church by joining her and changing her real identity and her ways.

The bishops of Rome, shortly after that time, began to exalt themselves as being chief in authority over all other ministers and churches. They supposed themselves to be the successors of Peter, but Peter's own written admonition to pastors had said just the opposite: "Neither as lords over God's heritage, but being examples to the flock." These Roman bishops also began to have the notion that they could actually forgive sins and that they were infallible in things pertaining to the faith.

WORMWOOD

The effect that these ungodly leaders had upon the church is described by the third trumpet as wormwood. This typifies bitterness. This experience for the church was similar to the Exodus of the children of Israel out of Egypt. After they were safely across the Red Sea, the first watering oasis they came to contained waters that were too bitter to drink.

And so this pretending star fell upon the rivers and fountains of pure gospel truth and made them bitter with untruths. God had opened these fountains for the purpose of cleansing from sin and uncleanness (Zechariah 13:1), but they became dark with the mud and filth of false teachings as ungodly pastors stirred them with unholy feet that had not been washed by the towel girded, kneeling Savior of sinners.

Rather than having the qualities of Christian humility, they sought after power and dominion, and the imperial church that followed them into the Dark Ages became a tool for obtaining political power at the cost of millions of human lives.

John tells us that this star fell upon the third part of the rivers and fountains. As we have already seen in the language of the third trumpet, this would apply to the third part of the population of the world that is descended from Japheth, one of Noah's three sons. These matters did not greatly affect the peoples of Africa or Asia, but they had tragic effect upon Europeans.

It further states that many men died because of the water. This is what happens when the way of salvation is not made clear. Sin encroaches upon men's lives, and early death can be the result. That is why James wrote, "Brethren, if any of you do err from the truth, and one convert him, let him know that he who converts the sinner from the error of his way shall save a soul from death, and shall hide a multitude of sins" (James 5:18-19). Bitter waters are an impossible remedy for a wasted and perishing life.

The time finally came when one could travel the breadth of the European continent and not find a place of open public worship that did not serve up these bitter waters. There was a remnant of churches, of course, that avoided this snare, but they were considered to be outside the law and were under constant persecution by the government and the Roman Church. And so the shades of superstition and carnal ambition began to be drawn as the evening of the Dark Ages descended upon the land of the Gentiles, which had waited so long for the light of eternal truth.

THE FOURTH TRUMPET

> *And the fourth angel sounded and the third part of the sun was smitten, and the third part of the moon, and the third part of the stars, so as the third part of them was darkened. And the day shone not for a third part of it, and the night likewise.* (Revelation 8:12)

The message of this fourth trumpet is darkness. It was within a hundred years from the time that the church became absorbed into the paganism of the Roman Empire that the cultural phenomenon that we know as the Dark Ages began to develop. This was a social and political disintegration that gradually swept all across the Western World and lasted for roughly five hundred years.

Numerous explanations have been offered as to the cause of it. The barbarian invasions into the empire were a factor that contributed to the cause of the decline of Roman civilization, but there was far more to the darkening process than just that. Some scholars have suggested that the Christian Church was responsible, but we Christians know that the exact opposite is true. The truth of God and Christ promotes the improvement of civilization, not the destruction of it. It is true, however, that the recognized church of Rome helped the process of degradation along, but that was a perverted church as we have seen and not a true one.

Here is a quotation by John Gill, a noted Baptist scholar of the eighteenth century. He applies this trumpet to the Dark Ages. "This trumpet has reference to that darkness and ignorance which the . . . barbarous nations, the Goths, Huns and Heruli spread and left throughout the empire; for from this time there was a visible decline as of evangelical light and knowledge, and nothing but stupidity and barbarity took place everywhere; and which was very assisting to the man of sin, Antichrist, to fix and settle his dominion over the kingdom which rose up out of the empire at this time."

Gill has reference to the Holy Roman Empire, which continued the Roman Empire for 1,260 years and which we will be noticing when we get to chapter 13 of Revelation. The facts are that from about the fifth to about the tenth or eleventh centuries the once-thriving cities and villages of the empire wasted away into a wretched and half-ruined state. Schools of learning became almost extinct. Literature was all but lost except among the monks, and rulers came to care little about perpetuating the high degree of Roman and Greek culture that had taken ages to develop.

In a way, it was a plague of darkness from God, sent against the apostate Roman Church, which ruled vast territories hand in hand with a revived but thoroughly corrupt Roman government. During the Middle Ages, from about AD 1000 to 1500, there was some improvement, but the real lifting of this plague of darkness did not come until the Protestant Reformation brought liberation to much of the church.

The symbols of the sun and moon being darkened have to be taken in biblical context. They are used in scripture sometimes to designate the powers that rule, as when Joseph in a dream saw his father and mother as the sun and moon and his brothers as twelve stars. In Joel chapter 2, they seem to have reference to the Jewish authority, which was about to crumble away—as Peter quoted from that chapter and applied it on the Day of Pentecost. During these Dark Ages, this is certainly what happened to rulers on the European continent. It was indeed a dark day for Gentile culture when compared to the brilliance of the Roman period that had preceded it.

We are also told that the third part of the day and night was darkened. Once again, the three divisions of the people of the earth come to mind. Again, the Roman Empire was a European entity, and Europe answers to a third part of the earth's three divisions—the third that was descended from Noah's son, Japheth.

Chapter 12

The Fifth Trumpet

The Book of Revelation is actually prophecy from God himself about what would be happening to his precious blood-bought church that he loves—during this age of Christianity. Now after about two thousand years of this age have passed, we can see that the prophecy has been unfolding in perfect order in the events that we call history.

In our study of these matters thus far, we have seen some of the events that happened early in our Gospel age, which, in Revelation, were represented by the sounding of trumpets. The first trumpet heralded the removal of the Jewish nation from the earthly kingdom of God (Matthew 21:43) and the utter destruction of their nation, which happened in the year AD 70. The second trumpet called out the spectacular growth and spread of the church among the Gentiles and the third was the descent of the greater part of that church (Roman Catholic) into its marriage with Roman paganism. The fourth trumpet was the descent of the Dark Ages upon the Western (Christian) World as God's retribution upon that apostasy.

As the centuries passed and the sounds of the fourth trumpet had faded away, the Western World was brought to the end of the Dark Ages. The previous thousand years had taken an awful toll upon Western civilization. The early church of Jesus Christ had largely been absorbed by a pagan religious culture and had been turned into a prison of legalism that used biblical language and traditions to mask its occult nature. It was high time for God to do something more, and he did. In three succeeding blasts, the fifth, sixth, and seventh trumpets announced more woe to the world with the words, "Woe, woe, woe."

WOE, WOE, AND MORE WOE

> *And I beheld, and heard an angel flying through the midst of heaven, saying with a loud voice, Woe, woe, woe to the inhabitants of the earth by reason of the other voices of the trumpet of the three angels which are yet to sound! And the fifth angel sounded, and I saw a star fall from heaven unto the earth, and to him was given the key of the bottomless pit. And he opened the bottomless pit, and there arose a smoke out of the pit, as the smoke of a great furnace. And the sun and the air were darkened by reason of the smoke of the pit. And there came out of the smoke locusts upon the earth, and unto them was given power, as the scorpions of the earth have power.* (8:13-9:3)

From the beginning of the Dark Ages until the time of the great Protestant Reformation a thousand years later, there had been no real change in the situation of the great ruling Catholic Church, except that it became increasingly more powerful and more forcefully resistant against any doctrine of practice that was not sanctioned by the government of the popes. But during that time, there were two major occasions in which an angry God confronted these backslidden Gentile peoples with two invading and destroying scourges.

THE RELIGION OF ISLAM

The first one was raised up in Arabia, and it flowed like a consuming tide toward Europe and its Holy Roman Empire that had been set up to accommodate Roman Catholicism and the perpetuation of a Roman Empire. These two entities ruled hand in hand over the European peoples for a long, long time.

Verse 1 of chapter 9 shows a "star" falling from heaven, and to "him" was given the key to the bottomless pit. Clearly, this is not a good star. There are good stars in the Bible, and there are bad stars. Jude speaks of some stars as "wandering stars for whom is reserved the blackness of darkness forever." Those stars are going to be sent into the lake of fire someday, indicating that they are people who are not of God's family. Demons can also be described as stars, and this star we are seeing is apparently a fallen angel. But not just any angel. He is an angel of very high degree. He is a demonic power high in the hierarchy of Satan, and he has the control of the key of the bottomless pit.

THE BOTTOMLESS PIT

The bottomless pit, by the way, is a phrase that occurs in the King James translation of the Bible, and it can also be translated as "the abyss." It is actually the same word that is translated in one of the Gospels as "the deep." One remembers the occasion when Jesus cast out the legion of devils from the Gadarene. They pleaded to him that he would not send them into "the deep." On that occasion, they were on the shore of the Sea of Galilee, but these demons were not speaking about that deep. In fact, when they were actually cast out of the man, they rushed into a herd of swine, causing them to run violently down a steep place into the sea, and were drowned. They did that because demons seem to be addicted to the destruction of flesh.

So it was not the actual water that they were referring to as "the deep." What they were asking was that Christ not send them back into the bottomless pit. The bottomless pit, or abyss, as it is also called in some translations, is apparently some kind of a holding tank for fallen angels. They are released from time to time and sent back into it from time to time.

The amazing thing about this is that God sometimes uses fallen angels to accomplish his tasks. There are occasions in Bible history when he used the services of fallen angels. For example, when God was ready to cause the downfall and death of King Ahaz of Israel, he used a demon of lying to go into Ahaz's prophets and produce lies against the king. Through these false prophecies, a demon promised Ahaz that he would have victory in battle, when actually he would be drawn into the battle and killed. Yes, God did that.

Also, when God was dealing with the man Job, he used the devil himself to accomplish certain things in order to show the fallen principalities and powers (fallen angels or demons) that Job was not going to fall or sin against his God—but would remain faithful. Of course, God knew that he would remain faithful, but to show the fact of Job's integrity and faithfulness, God used the evil intent and actions of Satan. And he continues to sometimes use evil angels in our present times to do his works, just as he uses his good angels as well.

So on this occasion in Revelation, we see a great number of demons being loosed out of the bottomless pit and going out into the world. Now when these devils go forth and do their work, they do it through natural means. Paul said in Ephesians, "We wrestle not against flesh and blood but against principalities and powers."

What he meant was that we normally think we are fighting against people, against situations, against things that come into our lives. And yes, we are doing that, but behind those apparently natural things—those natural people and events—there are fallen angels doing their work against us. God allows it and uses it. It is part of the warfare that is going on in this world that he will finish and accomplish when he sends his son from heaven. Then it will be all over.

THE FIRST WOE

What we have here in this fifth trumpet is the beginning of a major world religion that established its cause and presence through military invasions over a large part of the world. And that is the way false religions have often worked throughout time. At this point in time, the Dark Ages had come upon the lands of Europe. We saw that happening with the fourth trumpet. It was an expression of God's anger against the unholy alliance of the church and the Holy Roman Empire. But after all that God did in sending darkness over the once-glorious land of the Romans, nothing had really changed. Just because God may send a plague doesn't mean that people will acknowledge where it came from or the reason for it. Even though they suffer from it, they don't always learn the lessons that God intended for them. So nothing had changed except an awful decline in civilization.

Therefore, the prophet John here in Revelation declared three woes that would come after this. The first woe appeared upon the earth in the seventh century. It was the new religion of Islam. We know that there is much moral and practical good in all the religions of the world. However, there is only one way to a full relationship with God, and that is through the Lord Jesus Christ and the Holy Spirit. We Christians believe that. And there is no doubt that, historically, the rise of Islam was a terrific plague against Europe. In our history books, we read about this great conflict that occurred between Islam and Christianity and which has continued down through the centuries.

The Islamic religion began in the country of Arabia, and then it swept westward across Northern Africa. After it completely engulfed the northern part of Africa, it crossed over the Strait of Gibraltar there at the western end of the Mediterranean Sea and over into Spain. And then these Arabian Islamic zealots pressed on into France before they were finally stopped by forces under Charles Martel, a Christian leader who was the grandfather of Charlemagne—the first Holy Roman emperor. Historically, these Islamic peoples were called the Saracens, and there is much to the credit of this new religion and culture. It was not all bad although there was certainly a fear and dread of them in the European regions. This resulted in the spread of the great Islamic culture that still occupies a great portion of the earth's surface. These armies not only conquered and held a large part of the world, but they also developed a civilization and a culture that was really equal to Europe's at the time.

So these Saracen invaders waged their holy wars against all countries that were in their sight, and they won their wars everywhere they went. It took about 150 years for their military and religious expansion to finally come to an end.

LOCUSTS AND SCORPIONS

All through the Book of Revelation, various forms of living creatures are used to symbolically represent things that are actual and real. Just here we have two of them—*locusts and scorpions*. The animal life and the creatures that are used as symbols in the Bible tend to be particular animal forms that are actually found in the regions and countries that are prophetically under consideration.

Here in the language of the fifth trumpet of Revelation, these swarms of locusts are actually common to the Arabian countryside, where they can gather in huge numbers. But another reason for this usage is probably that they devour almost everything that grows, and they move in huge swarms, consuming as they go. In application, this was characteristic of the Saracen armies that destroyed the people of the countryside as they marched in their relentless consumption of the land—conquering such a large part of the earth's surface as they rode. And they routinely slew all who would not convert and confess their religion of Islam. Such were the instructions to them in their holy book, the Koran. Yes, the Koran teaches peace too, but only at the expense of conversion.

In Arabian culture, there is even a tradition repeated about some locusts that fell into the hand of Mohammed himself. He saw written on their bodies and on their wings the words, "We are the army of the most high God."

Then there is the mention of the scorpions. Scorpions are very painful in their stings, so this seems to speak about the painful sting of war that they carried on—the hard sting of bloodshed and death that accompanied it all.

This interpretation that we are following concerning the fifth and sixth trumpets is somewhat traditional with the older Bible expositors who wrote on the Book of Revelation. If you have access to a religious library, you may find this in some of the old commentaries such as John Gill, Albert Barnes, and Jamieson, Fausett and Brown. The newer commentaries will more likely give a futurist interpretation rather than a historicist one. The pendulum has swung in the interpretation of prophecy, just as it has in theology.

Understanding that Revelation takes us on a prophetic trip through time, we have made our journey from the very beginning of the church age through the times of the great outspread of the church—its descent into awful apostasy and marriage with paganism—through the Dark Ages of time, which was God's judgment on that apostasy—and now into the beginning of the three woes, which was, and still is today, God's further judgments upon that apostasy.

Now in chapter 9, we find ourselves in the seventh and eighth centuries AD, making our prophetic way into what we call the Middle Ages. In this chapter, we see the beginnings of the great Islamic religion and culture and their sudden warlike spread over North Africa, through Spain, and then into Europe as they invaded the lands of Christianity, intending to establish Islam as the only world religion. And that is still their aim today.

So as they invaded, the commandment was given for them to hurt only those men who did not have the seal of God on their foreheads.

> *And it was commanded them that they should not hurt the grass of the earth, neither any green thing, neither any tree, but only those men which have not the seal of God in their foreheads.* (Revelation 9:4)

This is a very important principal in the Word of God. We should understand that God was sending these Islamic armies against an apostate

European continent and, in particular, against those people who had desecrated his truth and had set up a human religious government in the name of the church—The Holy Roman Empire. God was not going to allow that to go on permanently.

THE INVISIBLE MARK

At that time, those true Christians who were still worshipping in spirit and in truth and who were against this Roman Catholic marriage between state and religion were marked by God for their preservation. This interesting fact about God's protection of his obedient people during times of warfare is made plain in the ninth chapter of Ezekiel. This remarkable passage of scripture shows how advancing human armies are preceded by destroying angels from God. But at the same time, he sends special angels to place a mark upon his obedient people to protect them from destruction. And angels still do that. When wars and plagues come to earth, we should realize as Christians that those who "sigh and cry for the abominations that are being committed in the land" (Ezekiel 9:4) have placed upon their foreheads, in plain sight of God's destroying angels, an invisible mark that protects them when the desolation comes raging through. This is one of many wonderful principles in the Bible about which Christian people tend to be ignorant, but thankfully, it is true. The world is not run by a system of chance, but rather by the plans of heaven and decrees of the almighty God who knows what he is doing.

So now, picking up in chapter 9 verse 4, we have a description of these invading armies. These events occurred in the seventh and eighth centuries.

> *And to them it was given that they should not kill them, but that they should be tormented five months. And their torment was as the torment of a scorpion, when he strikes a man.*

We have noticed the symbol of the locusts earlier, and they represented the great violent spread of these armies and this religion. In those days, invaders did not just single out combatants, but women and children as well, like the sting of scorpions.

Now it says that they should not kill them but should rather torment those against whom they were sent. We know that they went against

Christian Europe and the depraved, murdering Roman Church. And there were, of course, many people—thousands upon thousands—who were killed during those wars that lasted over a hundred years. But the real subject of God's wrath, which was the apostate church, was not killed, so perhaps this is what is meant by the command that they should not kill but should torment.

The church in power was certainly tormented by this Islamic scourge. But the roots of the Romanist religion in that part of the world were not crushed; they actually continued to grow even afterward although they were set back to some degree by these invasions.

FIVE MONTHS

And it says that they would torment them for five months. Let's see what that may mean. In interpreting Bible prophecy, we can often use 30 days as symbolic of a month. So there were 5 months, it says, and 5 times 30 would equal 150 days. Also, there is a tradition in the interpretation of Bible prophecy that a day can represent a year.

Now why does God do this? He does it to confuse the reader. Not the godly spiritual reader, who is able to prepare and learn, but for those who are not godly or spiritual. As we have noticed before, this is the same reasoning that Christ used in the giving of his parables. He told his disciples that he was not giving the parables to make things clearer, but rather to obscure meanings so that only those who had "ears to hear" could understand (Matthew 13:11). This is done in prophecy also, so we have do dig out the symbols and the codes. And there has to be a lot of prayer and study as well.

So the year that Mohammed actually began to preach was AD 612. So from AD 612 going forward in time for 150 years brings us to about the time that Baghdad was built. And at that time the armies of the Islamic Saracen Arabians stopped the main thrust of their outward spread and began giving themselves to internal matters and the building of their civilization. When that happened, Europe finally got a rest from the onslaught.

Now we come to verse 6: "And in those days shall men seek death and they shall not find it, they shall desire to die and death shall flee from them."

In a sense, perhaps, this is expressive of the Saracens' capture of Europeans to become slaves. In those cases, the slaves might well have preferred death to the abuses of slavery.

HOW THEY LOOKED

> And the shapes of the locusts where like unto horses prepared unto battle, and on their heads were as it were crowns of gold. And their faces were as the faces of men, and they had hair as the hair of women and their teeth were as the teeth of lions. And they had breastplates as it were breastplates of iron, and the sound of their wings were as the sound of chariots of many horses running into battle. And they had tails like scorpions. And there were stings in their tails, and their power was to hurt men for 5 months. (9:7-10)

Here we borrow an interpretation from another writer. This is from a book titled *The War with Satan* by English Bible scholar, Basil F. C. Atkinson. He writes that verses 7 through 10 of chapter 9 give us the description of the Saracen army, partly in language taken from the prophet Joel, who describes an invading army like them. These words are taken from Joel 1:6. They were like horses prepared for war. Here is the formidable strength of the Saracen armies. On their heads was something like crowns of gold. These are the yellow turbans worn by the Arabs. Their faces were like men's faces, and this refers to the beards worn by the Saracens. The Christians of Southern Europe were usually clean shaven at that time. And their hair was like that of women, which is also an accurate description of an Arab's appearance. Their hair fell down to their shoulders. And their teeth were like lions' teeth. This is fulfilled in the way the Saracens crushed and devoured their prey. They had breastplates like iron. This describes the armor that they wore. The apostle heard the noise of the locusts' wings, like the noise of chariot horses running to battle. This language again is taken from the prophet Joel and it well describes the rush of the Saracen armies. Thus interprets Basil Atkinson.

And then we come to verse 11: "And they had a King over them which is the angel of the bottomless pit, whose name in the Hebrew tongue is Abaddon, but in the Greek tongue has his name Apollyon."

THE RULING DEMON

Now why do we have this name given in two languages, Hebrew and Greek? Possibly because these two languages are involved in this process. The Hebrew language, because these horsemen overran the area of the world where Hebrew had been spoken. They overran Palestine, took it, and kept it. And in the Greek, because there was also much Greek territory that was taken by these armies. And both of these names mean destruction.

That obviously fits the case here. Also, this individual appears to be a ruling spirit—a high-level demon—one of the principalities and powers against which we struggle. He and his legions were in charge of this onrushing, destroying tide that God sent against the perverted Christian Church of the early Middle Ages.

Now this is just the first of these three woes seen here in Revelation. We will next see the second one revealed in the great spread of Islamic wars through the Ottoman Empire, which ended with World War I. Then the third and last woe will be the great stirring of warlike Islamic zeal in our own time—which many today call our "war on terror."

CHAPTER 13

The Sixth Trumpet

In previous chapters, we have heard and examined the first five blasts that have sounded forth from the seven trumpets of the Book of Revelation. They signified five major events that affected the church of Jesus Christ in her journey through this present and last age of time. Now we come now to the sixth trumpet in chapter 9, verse 13:

> *One woe is passed and behold there come two woes more hereafter. And the sixth angel sounded, and I heard a voice from the four horns of the golden altar which is before God.*

This is a prophetic description of next to the last one of these great formative events that have happened in our Gospel age. These are milestones for us to let us know how far down this last journey we have come. All these last three are heralds of woe. Also, the destructive forces of war that we saw in the fifth trumpet will continue into this one as well.

THE GOLDEN ALTAR

Why is the golden altar mentioned? A voice sounds from the four horns of the golden altar. And what was this altar? It was the altar of incense that was in the tabernacle in Old Testament times and later placed in the temple. Many have seen this unique altar as symbolic of the fervent prayers of God's people. The place where it stood was against the beautiful veil that separated the holy place from the holiest of all—the closest point that an ordinary priest could get to the awesome Ark of the Covenant, representing the very presence of God. Likewise, prayer, devotion, and the filling by the Spirit is the closest point to God that one may get in this present life.

God tells us in his Word to pray for his will to be done. In other words, the accomplishment of his will in the earth rests at least in part upon our praying for things to happen. Does that impress you? It should. God has literally brought us into his boardroom where decisions are made and actions are initiated. And we have to realize that these things happen because people pray for them.

During the Middle Ages, there were people all across Europe who were yearning and struggling to worship in freedom without the shackles of the Roman Catholic system upon them. And they were praying, just like people are praying in countries of oppression today, for deliverance and freedom. And God always sends that deliverance in his good time. When times came for these prayers of deliverance to be answered, he sent these three *woe* trumpets. And as they destroyed and rearranged the political structure of Europe, there was also a releasing effect upon the people of Europe who were under oppression during those times.

Verse 14: "Saying to the sixth angel which had the trumpet, loose the four angels which are bound in the great river Euphrates. And the four angels were loosed which were prepared for an hour, and a day, and a month, and a year for to slay the third part of men."

ISLAM ON THE MOVE AGAIN

Here we have another military invasion against Europe that was very similar to the one preceding it. And here we can rely upon some traditional interpretation. Excellent Bible scholars have written on this sixth trumpet. Some of them were Martin Luther, Joseph Need, John Napier, Sir Isaac Newton, Jonathan Edwards, and John Wesley. All of them have identified this sixth trumpet as being symbolic of the forces of Islam. But this time, it was not under the Arabs. It was under the Turks and the great Ottoman Empire—a tremendous far-reaching military and political force that that lasted even into our modern times. Notice that these angels that were loosed had been bound in the river Euphrates. Therefore, we have to apply this to the part of the world where the Euphrates River flows.

About the year AD 1057, a vast horde of Turkish tribesmen from Central Asia appeared on the banks of the Euphrates River in their westward migratory march. As they expanded into the Middle East, they adopted the Islamic religion and, in the fire of it, began to replace the Arabians as the rulers of the Islamic lands. These Turks were even more cruel and intolerant than the Arabians had been. Their barbarous treatment of the Christians in Palestine led to the Crusades that occurred from about AD 1095 to 1272. And for almost three hundred years, there was intermittent war in which the European Christians tried to regain the Holy Land from these Turkish Muslims.

The river Euphrates is there in the present country of Iraq. That is, in the area where old Babylon and the Babylonian Empire used to be. And in a sense, both historically and geographically, it constitutes a part of the dividing line between the Eastern and Western worlds. So here we have a gate, as it were, which separated East from West. But the times were coming for this gate to be opened and for mighty things to happen.

The angels, as we saw previously, were some of Satan's destroying angels. So here they were again, accumulating power and force under the permission and orders of God himself and bringing to pass great events in world history. These four angelic powers, of course, worked through men who were in positions of governmental, religious, and military power. They particularly worked through four areas of power there in the early stages of the Ottoman Empire. The seats of these Turkish power centers were Aconiam, Baghdad, Alepho, and Damascus—four of them—with one of the four angels probably assigned to each one.

Then we are given the duration of time in which they were to do their work. We see in verse 15 that they were prepared for an hour, a day, a month, and a year to slay a third part of men. Remember that God has given us the symbol of a day to represent a year, and this works in some Bible prophecies, but not all.

We will lay that aside for the moment. The day ("prepared for a day") would be a year. Prepared for a month, with 30 days to the month, would be 30 years. And then a year, if we take 365 days to a year, would be 365 years. So adding all these together, we have 365 days, which become 365 years; plus 30 days, which become 30 years; plus 1 day, which becomes a year. This gives us a total of 396 years plus a fraction or a portion of a year.

Now in my own research of this, there are three authors, Bible commentators, who have interpreted all this in one way and a couple of others who have given it in another. Some give 365 days for a year and some use 360 days for a year. I am going to use the 365 days for a year since it works more perfectly.

So here, then, is how the dates work out. In the year 1057, the Turkish Empire began its first military expedition westward, and then 396 years later (this is the period of time that we just added up from the prophecy) brings us to the year 1453. *On that very year,* Constantinople, the capital of the Eastern Roman Empire, fell to the advancing Ottoman Turks. And in that sense, God's judgment against the Eastern Roman Empire was completed.

THE SULTAN'S LAST SALLY

After this, of course, the Ottoman Turks continued their invasion of Europe, and they began to press against the Western Roman Empire until the year 1529. This date does not seem to have a significance in prophecy, but I think it is interesting. In 1529, they had worked their advance with unusually large armies, all the way westward to the city of Vienna. And it was there at the gates of Vienna that they were finally stopped by forces of the Holy Roman Empire, and that was as far as they got into Europe on that occasion. One historian called it the sultan's last sally. For several months now, we have been examining the trumpets of the Book of Revelation and applying them to past events of world history. We are using this old respected method of interpretation rather than the popular one that is used today to apply these prophetic trumpets to our future. Now here are other remarkable evidences. In verse 16, we are given the size of this huge army of Turks:

> *And the number of the army and the horsemen were two hundred thousand thousand. And I heard the number of them.*

This is two hundred million men. This is larger than any army that has ever marched in the world's entire history. Actually, there were some very large armies that were fielded in earlier times. Armies back in that time, in fact, tended to be larger than armies are today—and were more compacted. At the siege of Vienna, previously mentioned, there were 250,000 Turks that came against Vienna on that occasion. A few other times, armies fielded as many as 400,000 men at one time during that period. But we don't know of any particular battle or occasion in which this many men, 200 million, were actually in the field at one time.

But God here is not necessarily obligated to give us the number of men involved in any one battle. All this conflict occurred over a period of about 396 years, if the prophetic counting that we just did is correct. Now considering all the armies that did march from the Turkish Empire at that time, all the battles that were waged, all the men that went through the armed forces—then we might find (if we had that information) that the total of all the soldiers that the Turkish army contained may well have been two hundred million men over that whole period of time. The important thing is that God knows how many there were, and perhaps that is the figure he is giving us.

So we come to verse 17: "And thus I saw the horses in the vision, and them that sat on them, having breastplates of fire, and of jacinth, and brimstone. And the heads of the horsemen were as the heads of lions, and out of their mouths issued fire and smoke and brimstone."

Although this is symbolic language, it is strikingly close to what one would have actually seen as he might have watched this attacking Muslim army. The breastplates that were used by the Turks were of polished iron and glistened in the sun. Also, colored armor was used at that time, and they would have stood out as one observed them in battle. To the writer, the horses' heads appeared similar to lions' heads because these cavalrymen used plumes on their horses' heads to make them appear larger than normal. The plumes were a symbol of honor among these Turkish tribesmen.

Verse 18: "By these were the third part of men killed by the fire, and by the, smoke and by the brimstone, which issued out of their mouths."

This is an amazing fulfillment of the prophetic description. This was the first time in the history of the Western World when large armies used gunpowder and firearms in major battles. Dr. Halley, in his *Bible Handbook*, makes this comment, "The Eastern Roman Empire (395-1453), its capital, Constantinople, had, for centuries (AD 630-1453) been the bulwark of European defense against Mohammedanism. But in AD 1453 it fell to the Turks. It was at the battle of Constantinople (AD 1453) that artillery with gunpowder was first used, which gave victory to the Turks; the fire, smoke and brimstone of 9:17." Therefore, we have as it says in

Revelation, the fire, smoke, and brimstone appearing to issue out of the mouths of the horsemen.

Then we read that the third part of men was killed by these things. There are a couple of interpretations about this that we have already seen. But quite often the word "third" means Europe or Western Europe, especially that part that was under the old Roman Empire. It could mean that during this period of time, almost four hundred years, there was actually a third part of the inhabitants, who were living in that area, who were killed in these wars. At any rate, there were huge numbers of men who were slain during these battles between the two empires, which were waging war. It was a hard and furious contest against each other for such a long, long time. Then we have in verse 20 this strange and pathetic statement:

> *And the rest of the men who were not killed by these plagues yet repented not of the works of their hands, that they should not worship devils, and idols of gold, and silver, and brass, and stone, and wood, which neither can see, nor hear, nor walk.*

What does this mean, "the rest of the men"? This must mean those who were not killed—those who were at home who did not go to the battles and who continued just as they were before—living in the same continued idolatry and sins that had caused all this in the first place.

As far as beneficial effects that this trumpet, these destructive invasions, had upon Europe, they did give the struggling Christians who wanted to be free some breathing space. During this period of time, the Great Protestant Reformation was taking place. And if the armies of the Holy Roman Empire had not had to divide themselves against this advancing Eastern force, they would have had more time to crush the Protestant Reformation. So God sent the scourge at just the right time.

The phrase "the rest of the men" would include, then, the supporters of the official Catholic Church in the Western Roman Empire. The fact was, and it is historically evident if anyone cares to read the record, that the Holy Roman Empire was extremely corrupt during these times. Once again, from *Halley's Bible Handbook*, we read, "Boniface VIII, pope from 1294 until 1303, proclaimed, 'We declare, affirm, define, pronounce that it is altogether necessary for salvation that every creature be subject to the Roman Pontiff.' He himself was so corrupt that Dante, who visited

Rome during his pontificate, called the Vatican a 'sewer of corruption' and assigned him, along with Nicholas III and Clement V to the lowest parts of hell."

The last thing we want to notice about this trumpet is that the star fell upon the third part of the rivers and fountains. We have already seen in previous language (in the second trumpet) that this expression one-third applies to the third part of the world's population that had descended from Japheth, one of Noah's three sons.

These events that were taking place at that time did not greatly affect people who were living in Africa, Asia, or the Americas, but they were very vital issues to the Europeans who were dwelling in the isles or coastlands. *Isles* is the prophetic code word in the Old King James Bible for lands that bordered the northern part of the Mediterranean Sea. So during that time, a third part of the world—the European descendants of Japheth—suffered the first and second woes, which were the awful two invasions from the Islamic East and South.

Chapter 14

The Three Woes and the Seventh Trumpet

The Book of Revelation is probably as popular now among Christians as it has ever been in the life of the church. Two factors that have contributed to this popularity would be our passing the benchmark year, AD 2000, and also having new books about the end of time flooding our bookstores and even being made into action horror movies.

The bad side of this is that this new popularity of Revelation isn't helping us very much to understand the times in which we are living. The big modern trend that is being followed in interpreting this great prophetic book is to apply all of it to an end-time "tribulation" period of seven years *that has not yet started*—and in the opinion of many Bible students, never will. What a loss of useful, practical information this is.

ALWAYS SOMETHING NEW

The people of our present generation are somewhat akin to the citizens of Athens at a time when the Apostle Paul was passing through their city. We read in the Book of Acts that they spent their time in doing nothing else but to hear and to tell some new thing. Paul used that occasion to preach some basic Gospel to them, and he even referred them back to a statement that had been made by one of their own philosophers. But apparently they didn't think that the old writers of the past were very important. And so is with us today.

If we were interested enough to check out the older writers of commentaries on the Book of Revelation, we would find a very different story from the one that is now being told in the bookstores and on the movie screens.

For one thing, the old guys took a more practical approach to prophetic interpretation. They believed that Revelation is actually *prophecy about our entire Gospel-church age* (two thousand years of history now) and not about just a few short desperate years that would come at the end of it all. *They actually pinpointed certain passing historical events as being the fulfillment of the visions of Revelation.*

THE FIRST WOE

The fifth and sixth trumpets are especially meaningful to us today because they began a sequence of events that Revelation calls the three woes (8:13). According to the old writers, the fifth trumpet announced the arrival of the religion of Islam upon the world scene and its phenomenal spread over large parts of the earth. This was during the seventh and eighth centuries when the Arabs conquered territory from Arabia all the way across Northern Africa and even through Spain and into France. They were plunging toward the heart of Europe from the west when they were finally stopped. As we have been observing, the language in Revelation about this fifth trumpet is striking in its description of the Arabian hordes in their conquests.

Just as the fourth trumpet (Dark Ages) had represented God's judgment upon the fall of the outward church into apostasy, this fifth trumpet heralded his judgment upon a church that had become drunk with power. During this particular time, the first real pope had been crowned and his kingship declared among the other kings of the earth. There was also the new unholy marriage of power between the pope and the emperors of the Holy Roman Empire. God knows how to punish people for their sins, and this scourge against Christian Europe was exactly that.

THE SECOND WOE

Next, the sixth trumpet (second woe) declared the same thing all over again. By this time, the Turks had become the invincible leaders of Islam, and in the seventeenth century, they plunged toward Christian Europe again—this time from the east. They got all the way to the gates of Vienna, Austria, before they were finally stopped. They formed the mighty Ottoman Empire, which lasted, in fact, until World War I. Was this also a judgment from God, and if so, for what purpose? During these times, Europe was enveloped in the throes of the great Protestant Reformation. The Protestants were holding out mainly in the northern part of Europe, and the Islamic scourge came up from the south. This allowed a struggling European Protestant Church to gain some breathing space from the counterattacking Roman Catholic forces. Had it not been for this pressure and invasion from Islam, the Protestant Reformation might well have been crushed.

This sounds as if God used the mighty religion of Islam for a good purpose, does it not? Well, do you suppose he still might be doing that? These two Islamic invasions were pictured as woes in Revelation 8:13, and they were indeed that. These bloody invasions sent shivers through all of Europe in those days, and if God had not stopped them, there would be no Christianity left on the earth today.

THE THIRD WOE

But this is not all there is. There were actually three of these woes described in Revelation, not just two. The third one does not appear until chapter 11, verses 14-15, and there it is found in conjunction with the end of our age:

> *The second woe is past, and behold the third woe comes quickly. And the seventh angel sounded, and there were great voices in heaven saying, the kingdoms of this world are become the kingdoms of our Lord and of His Christ, and He shall reign forever and ever.*

I think it is safe to say that a lot of Christians (maybe most) think that we are living at the end of our age and that Christ will return again soon. Certainly we have seen these several prophecies in this book all running out at once during these modern times of ours. When Christ does return, he will take over all the governments of our world, just as the verse above describes. But notice that there is another woe connected to these times. The first two woes were about the losing of Islamic invasions against a Christian world that was delving deeply into apostasy. Could it be that this is the same scenario of this last third woe and the seventh trumpet?

Consider the times we are now living in. The major conflict on our world today is between the Islamic and Christian nations. The "war on terror" has now replaced the "cold war" with Russia that lasted for so long. And this time the land and people of Israel are involved as well. Actually, it doesn't really make any sense. Why do the Palestinians continue to attack Israel knowing that they are greatly outclassed militarily? And why do the Islamic terrorist groups keep attacking the citadels of Christianity knowing they cannot win any real military confrontations? Something has stirred up these people and given them a renewed cause to fight for again. The Islamic demon prince called Abaddon in chapter 9 has reactivated his forces once again, just as Bible prophecy indicated he would.

ISLAM ON MISSION

A possible answer to this present and building conflict between East and West is that the God of heaven has sent the Muslim people out on a mission again. They may actually be sent to purge the Christian Church in our time. But for what possible reason, we may ask? Isn't this the great Christian America that they are messing with? Who do they think they are? Yes, we can ask these questions, but people who are on a mission from God do not ask questions; they just go. On the first two occasions when the Islamic peoples invaded Christian Europe, their comparative power to wage war was approximately equal with the West's, so after much prolonged agony on both sides, there was finally a standoff. But today, the two sides are not equal. The Christian West far outstrips the Middle East militarily, economically, and in many other ways. They cannot engage in a military confrontation with the West and win, so they are doing what North Vietnam did and are waging a guerilla war that is being far more successful than we would have believed it could be. So why are they being so resolute and aggressive? Could they be on another mission from the Lord because of a spirit of apostasy that has encroached upon the lands of Christianity?

Therefore, we need to ask ourselves some questions. Does Christian America and Christian Europe need purging? Let's examine ourselves. What is the state of Christianity in our land? There is actually a great division that *nobody wants to talk about, and it amounts to another reformation in our time*. It is a great divisive force in Christ's kingdom today, just as the Protestant Reformation was divisive a few centuries ago.

This division has shown up all across the spectrum of Christianity in the Western World. Here in America it has effectively split the Presbyterian Churches into two parts not many years ago. It is tearing at the fabrics of the Episcopal and the Methodist churches. It has divided the great Southern Baptist Convention into two parts, even though that fact is not officially recognized. Not many years ago, leaders of Bible-believing Baptists had to launch a major offensive to regain control of Baptist seminaries and even the denomination itself. This bold move has left the humanist-minded Baptists crying foul to this day. Some writers are calling this an apostolic reformation because it is a matter of either following the truths and patterns set forth by the original apostles or not doing it.

NEW APOSTOLIC REFORMATION

This great conflict is being played out between authentic scriptural Christianity that has weathered the centuries until now *and a compromised humanistic Christianity that denies miracles, denies prophecy, the work of the Holy Spirit, the virgin birth, and much of the Holy Bible.* This is a genuine new reformation of great magnitude that is in progress now in our generation. God cares about what Christians believe, and he has his ways of bringing us back around to a purer state and condition.

So what effect has the Islamic *third woe* or reign of terror had upon this new Christian reformation? For one thing, it has rallied more Christians to action. The destruction of the World Trade Center in New York City was the major wake-up call, and the wars against Afghanistan and Iraq have intensified the issue. Recent governmental elections have shown us how the Apostolic Reformation is carried over into our political arena. This was also true of the first two woes. They were very political in nature to be sure as wars are always political. And before the real conflict will be over finally, the liberal agenda and effort to keep religion out of politics will come to failure, and the world will come to see that God's hand is in it all.

The humanists of our time (both secular and Christian humanists) know all about this reformation, and they want to keep it out of politics. They call out for a sharp dividing line to be drawn between church and state so that there will be no vestige of religion left at all in political life. That would be to their advantage, of course. They want to keep this conflict as quiet as possible because they work and accomplish best under cover.

But we may be seeing a new trend developing. As conservatism gains ground in the worlds of politics and education here in America, it may also make more gains in the world of the church. Bible-believing Christians must recognize what is happening and be willing to speak out for biblical truth in the marketplace of ideas just as Paul did in the city of Athens (Acts 17). God commands his people to come out of systems of unbelief and to stand upon his revealed Word (Revelation 18:4).

HEAVEN OPENED

Now we should notice that the scripture above, Revelation 11:14, makes a direct connection between the third woe and the return of Christ our king. This prophecy plainly refers to the return of our Lord. Then in Revelation 19:11, we see preparations for his arrival given to us in symbolic form:

> *And I saw heaven opened, and behold a white horse, and He who sat upon him was called Faithful and True, and in righteousness he does judge and make war.*

There is a widespread belief that this will be the physical return of Jesus Christ to the earth. However, the language is still symbolic, and the rider upon the white horse is called the Word of God, just as we have seen him in the first seal. I myself believe that chapter 18 in its historic sequence shows us God working to clean up the residue of false worship all around the world, a work that greatly increased after the Protestant Reformation was over. Then, as we proceed to the rider on the white horse in chapter 19, this culminated in the intense evangelical fervor that came after World War II as this evangelistic spirit leaped across the Pacific Ocean and began spreading through the Far East on its way back to Jerusalem. Will it make its way east to west all around the world in two thousand years?

Then at the end of chapter 19, we read, "And I saw the beast, and the Kings of the Earth and their armies, gathered together to make war against Him who sat on the horse and against his army. And the beast was taken, and with him the false prophet that wrought miracles before him, with which he deceived those which had received the mark of the beast and those who worshipped the image. These both were cast alive into a lake of fire burning with brimstone."

What about these kings of the earth in verse 19? Perhaps this refers to the many wars of the twentieth century, especially the two big ones. And perhaps the United States and her allies are seen pictured in the person on the horse (the Word of God) and his army. These awful wars of this bloody century just past were not just wars in support of freedom and democracy. They were all about the righteousness and authority of our Lord Jesus Christ and the powers of heaven that were pitted against Satan, the beast, and rebellion against God's authority. Even today, I believe his army is made up of the armed forces of the United States and our allies. There is yet a big war to come, and we followers of Christ know who the victor will be.

We will return to these end chapters with some more thoughts about the very end and even the time afterward. We have seen time and events rolling along in order as the seven trumpets blasted forth their messages. At the end of chapter 9, this passage of time came to a pause and will not continue until chapter 18. The chapters between might be called the special feature section of the Book of Revelation—this Gospel age seen from several important perspectives. First, what will happen to the Word of God? Here is the answer to that question in more prophetic language.

Chapter 15

The Two Witnesses

The subject of chapter 11 of Revelation is, as Isaiah lamented in an age long before John lived, "Who has believed our report? And to whom is the arm of the Lord revealed?" It is a prophetic literary description of what would be happening to the Word of God during our long Gospel age. It answers the questions posed by Isaiah about who would believe and follow God and who would not. The chapter begins this way:

> *And there was given me a reed like unto a rod, and the angel stood, saying, rise, and measure the temple of God, and the altar, and those who worship therein. But the court which is without the temple leave out, and measure it not; for it is given unto the Gentiles, and the holy city shall they tread under foot forty and two months.* (Revelation 11:1-2)

John is instructed to measure the temple of God using a reed as a standard. The reed seems to be the Holy Scriptures, which are our standard. They are sometimes called a rod or rule (Psalm 110:2), and they are the only true measurement for God's people. The temple as set forth here seems to be the practicing, believing church of the age, of which the Jewish temple was a type or shadow. Or today we would say model. Paul said of the church that it is "built upon the foundations of the apostles and prophets, Jesus Christ Himself being the chief corner stone; in whom all the building fitly framed together grows unto a holy temple in the Lord" (Ephesians 2:20-21).

The temple of the Israelites is shown to us in the Hebrew letter as representing Christ and the church, and it is a great and rewarding study. The temple proper was never entered except by those who were sanctified into the priesthood, and likewise, only the elect of God of every nation—true believers in God and Christ—can ever enter the true church.

The outer court, however, was a different matter, for people other than priests could enter that place, and we see it here being given over to the nations of the Gentiles for them to tread under their feet. The word *Gentile* here would refer symbolically to people who are spiritually uncircumcised or unregenerate—not elect of God and born again. In essence, it can be said that many people who are Christians by profession never see anything but the outer aspects of the church, never entering into that sanctified holy place where only the called and chosen of God may go. In fact, for a long period of time during the Middle Ages, the only officially recognized church was one which consisted only of an "outer court," which had been delivered into the hands of Satan and false Christians for a period of *forty-two months*.

FORTY-TWO MONTHS

How long is this period of forty-two months? In order to properly fit this span of time into the events recorded here and proven by history, it is necessary once again to apply the *year for a day* principle. Since God has given us prophecy in coded form, it is necessary for us to use the devices he has given us in his Word to decipher the codes. The prophetic use of exchanging days for years and years for days can be seen in scriptures such as Numbers 14:34 and Ezekiel 4:6, as well as in 1 Peter 3:8.

Now 42 months at 30 days to the month is 1,260 days, which thus becomes 1,260 years. That's a long time! When could the church have been delivered into the hands of the ungodly for such a period of time? When the Lord Jesus Christ issued the great commission to his apostles, he warned them about coming severe persecutions, which would often be the results of their labors to preach the Word of God to an unbelieving Roman Empire. As we know, that happened. During the first two hundred years of church history, the Roman government horribly persecuted Christians.

This persecution was sporadic but continuous. Christian graves in the catacombs of Rome, dating from that era, are variously estimated at between two and seven *million*. But the amazing fact is that despite this intense opposition, the church did grow by huge numbers so that by the year 300, possibly one-third of the empire was secretly or openly Christian.

By that time, the trend was for the Roman government to begin relenting in persecuting the church and even favoring it in some ways. The emperor Constantine issued his Edict of Toleration in the year AD 313, granting religious liberty to all worshipers. The previous year, in 312, he had reportedly seen a vision of the cross suspended in the sky above the setting sun, and above it the words, "IN THIS SIGN CONQUER." There are many factors that tell us that this was not a sign from God, not that God doesn't go to war at times, but the wars that the Roman Empire began to wage from that time onward began to turn against the true church and to establish a false church system that was more pagan than it was truly Christian.

What happened at this time was that Satan joined the church. Admittedly, this is a strange statement to make, but observe what actually happened. Satan had been fighting against the Church since its inception and had only experienced failure despite the oceans of blood that had been spilled. It may have been the devil himself who invented the expression "If you can't beat them, join them" because this is just what he did. And the result was that he was much more successful in devastating the church and preventing the spread the Word of God from within than he had ever been from without.

The Church of Jesus Christ is, among other things, a place of separation for God's children from the evil elements of the world. When the church joins the world, it becomes, like fallen Babylon, "the habitation of devils, and the hold of every foul spirit, and a cage of every unclean and hateful bird" (Revelation 18:2).

This is possibly what Christ meant when he gave the parable of the grain of mustard seed, warning the church against sinking her roots into the world and growing huge branches for the resting place of filthy, spiritually unwashed creatures. Soon after this, the persecutions by the Roman government ceased. Laws were later passed to make church membership actually compulsory, thus opening the doors wide for individuals to enter who had no real spirit of repentance or belief and who knew nothing of the new birth.

This takeover of the rule of the church by seekers of political power was gradual but complete, and it lasted from the fourth century until the Protestant Reformation brought welcomed deliverance in the sixteenth century. It began with the Dark Ages, and it is no wonder they were dark. Martin Luther described the devil as the prince of darkness grim, and this prince was ruling with a very free hand until the arm of the Lord was finally bared and brought deliverance in his own appointed time.

THE TWO WITNESSES

> *And I will give power unto my two witnesses, and they shall prophesy a thousand two hundred and threescore days, clothed in sackcloth. These are the two olive trees, and the two lampstands standing before the God of the earth.* (Verses 3-4)

During this age of darkness, God's two witnesses were going to prophesy. Who are they? These two symbols represent the Word of God, as seen in the two testaments—Old and New. They are also called the two olive trees and two lampstands and are described in that way in the fourth chapter of Zechariah, where it says (verse 14), "These are the two anointed ones that stand by the Lord of the whole earth."

Zechariah was told, "This is the Word of the Lord unto Zerubbabel, saying not by might, nor by power, but by my spirit, says the Lord of Hosts."

All those devoted disciples of Christ who hid, worshipped God, and fought the monster church during this period of time could not bring about by their power or might needed deliverance until the Spirit of the Lord began to move in the hearts of Christians in such a way that the Word of God became like a spreading fire that moved across the continent. Then the light of the Reformation and the Renaissance began to dawn upon a spiritually and culturally devastated Europe. God's Words are spirit and life, and they are a perpetual witness, prophesying of the power of God in salvation as well as his vengeance upon the wickedness of man.

During this period of time, these two witnesses were to prophesy in sackcloth. This seems to represent their diminished state under persecution. One might say that they were in a condition of mourning for an unbelieving world, and yet their great power continued to be felt in retribution against those who fought against them.

> *And if any man will hurt them, fire proceeds out of their mouth, and devours their enemies. And if any man will hurt them, he must in this manner be killed. These have power to shut heaven, that it rain*

> *not in the days of their prophecy: and have power over waters to turn them to blood, and to smite the earth with all plagues, as often as they will.* (Verses 5 and 6)

No man has ever prevailed against God's Word. It testifies that the soul that sins shall die and that everything that is prophesied in them shall come to pass. There was a dearth of the Gospel during this age in which the church was being trampled by unregenerate feet. The bright clouds and showers of gospel truth and blessing that were promised to the church in Zechariah 10:1 and also by Christ in John 7:37 were largely held back from an apostate world.

> *And when they shall have finished their testimony, the beast that ascends out of the bottomless pit shall make war against them, and shall overcome them, and kill them.* (Verse 7)

Even before Martin Luther took his momentous stand, there was a stirring of pure religious fervor in the lands of the empire. As early as the year 1208, a crusade was ordered by the pope against numerous dissenters called Albigenses in northern Italy. After this, the opposition grew until it burst out forcefully in what we know now as the Protestant Reformation. The persecutions during this advance period were horrible, Satan fighting fiercely against the Word and each time appearing to be successful until some new dissension erupted in another place.

> *And their dead bodies shall lie in the street of the great city, which spiritually is called Sodom and Egypt, where also our Lord was crucified.* (Verse 8)

The Roman Church appeared to be victorious against all opposition during these pre-Reformation years. The city in which the apparently lifeless bodies of the two witnesses lay was Rome as it succeeded in the power and concept of the Roman Empire all through this extended period. It was the same city under whose authority Christ had been crucified, and it is further identified in Revelation 17:9. Satan, who had made his sixth try at world domination through use of the Roman Empire, was continuing this phase of his work through the extended Holy Roman Empire and the Roman Church.

> *And they of the people and kindreds and tongues and nations shall see their dead bodies three days and a half, and shall not allow their dead bodies to be put in graves.* (Verse 9)

How long is this three days and a half? I will offer this view only as a possibility for your consideration, but it seems a significant one to me. There was a fairly well-defined period of restlessness and testing of Roman Church power during the time from the Albigensian upheaval down to the start of the Reformation. This era was about 350 years long in which the Word of God did indeed seem to be dead and the Roman Church was victorious in keeping the Bible as the sole property of the Roman clergy—not to be let out to any of the common people—much less the horrible dissenters.

As we attempt to decipher God's prophetic codes, we can try various possibilities to see whether they work or not. Perhaps a day in this case corresponds to the round number of a hundred years, even as it represents other lengths of time in other parts of the scriptures.

Therefore, three and one-half days would be 350 years. Indeed, the Word of God did appear to be dead to the general population for that long, and yet the *peoples and kindreds and tongues and nations*, identified frequently in Revelation as God's true believers, would not allow that Word to be buried out of sight and forgotten. They continued, time and again, to resurrect it as it were until the Reformation gave the Word of God back to the people.

> *And they that dwell upon the earth shall rejoice over them, and make merry, and shall send gifts one to another, because these two prophets tormented they that dwell on the earth.* (Verse 10)

The language here tells us exactly what happened toward the end of this period. And when did it end? When was the 1,260 year period of unrighteous church rule finished? We know it ended with the Reformation, but when was that? Well, Luther nailed his 95 theses on the door of the church at Wittenberg in the year 1517, and this date is often used to mark the beginning of the Reform Movement. However, the outer court (or outer manifestation of the church) was not actually delivered out of Satan's ruling grasp until the Reform Movement had actually become effective in delivering large numbers of people from false worship.

In order to find the right date for this, we might search for an apex—the point at which papal opposition stopped gaining ground and actually began losing. Such a date would be August 24, 1572. At this time, there happened the worst single act of persecution of the entire struggle. It was, in a way, similar to the very worst hour of a critically ill person—after it is over, things finally begin to be better. On this one day alone in 1572, after vigorous urging by Pope Pius IV, about seventy thousand Huguenots—French Protestants—were slain by the French crown on behalf of the Roman Church.

This infamous event is called the St. Bartholomew's Day Massacre. When news of this horrible accomplishment reached Rome, there was great rejoicing there. The pope and his College of Cardinals staged a parade. A medal was struck, commemorating the event, and a cardinal dispatched to Paris to congratulate the King and Queen Mother.

Now read once again the language of verse 10 above, and notice how fitting that description is of the St. Bartholomew's Day Massacre and its results. Remember that it had long been the policy of the Romanist Church—and especially in that day—to prevent Bible reading and interpretation among the ordinary people so that the priesthood could maintain its power and authority. The Word of God, which says that man shall live by faith, is always a torment to man-made priestly organizations.

THREE AND ONE-HALF DAYS

> *And after three days and a half the Spirit of life from God entered into them, and they stood upon their feet, and great fear fell upon those who saw them.* (Verse 11)

This brings us to the end of the 1,260 year period. The Reformation Movement was the greatest single event to have occurred thus far in this Gospel age. As it began to spread, the fear of God fell upon vast numbers of Europeans whose forebears had languished under an enforced Gospel blackout. The Word of God actually rose to its feet and began to stir the hearts of men as only it can. Then the outer court of the church was delivered from the hands of the spiritually uncircumcised, and it all occurred in God's duly appointed time. And keep in mind that this prophecy was written about the year AD 90.

Now notice this—that from the year 312 when Constantine had his vision and Satan "joined the church" until the year 1572 when the tide of Romanist opposition to the Reformation turned at the St. Bartholomew's Day Massacre, a period of 1,260 years had elapsed (1572 minus 312 = 1,260). This 1,260 years corresponds to the 1,260 years or 42 months during which the holy city would be trodden underfoot.

And what is the holy city? We read in Hebrews, "But you are come unto Mount Zion, and unto the city of the Living God, the heavenly Jerusalem, and to an innumerable company of angels, to the general assembly and *church* of the firstborn" (12:22). Notice that this church of Christ the firstborn is called the *heavenly* Jerusalem. The word *heaven* sometimes appears in the scriptures representing the visible, worshipping church of God. As the Word of God began to exert its power over reformed and freed Christian lives, this is what happened, in prophetic language:

> *And they heard a great voice from heaven saying unto them, Come up hither. And they ascended up to heaven in a cloud, and their enemies beheld them.* (Verse 12)

Here is God's Word ascending once again into prominence among visibly organized churches. This Word cannot be killed, for it will accomplish all that for which it is sent. Nor can the church be slain, for the gates of shall not prevail against it. Together, the Word and the church are enough to shake the earth, and they have done so on more than one occasion. We read also in Hebrews that it was God "whose voice then shook the earth: but now He has promised, saying, yet once more I shake not the earth only, but also heaven. And this Word, yet once more, signifies the removing of those things that were shaken, as of things that are made, that those things which cannot be shaken may remain" (Hebrews 12:26-27).

Just as God shook the earth (nations and rulers) and heaven (the organized temple worship or church) during and after the time of the apostles, so it happened once again when the Reformation came to shake Europe.

> *And the same hour was there a great earthquake, and the tenth part of the city fell, and in the earthquake were slain of men seven thousand. And the remnant were frightened, and gave glory to the God of heaven.* (Verse 13)

It is most apparent that the Reformation struck Europe like a gigantic earthquake, one in which untold thousands of people were slain in religious wars and hideous persecutions. When the shaking finally subsided and the air began to clear, there emerged a remnant of severely frightened souls—men and women whose fear of God and to do evil was a great part of the foundation upon which a newly progressive and enlightened Northern Europe came into being. Had it not been for this revival of the Word of God in the Reformation Movement, there would be no religious freedom as we know it today nor would there be the freedom of thought and invention that has so blessed our modern world.

Chapter 16

The Lady and the Dragon

Thus we come to the end of the first special feature chapter in Revelation. We have seen the fortunes of the Bible, the Word of God, as the centuries of this church age have passed. The next chapter contains the next special feature, and it will reveal for us the fortunes of the church.

At the base of the Statue of Liberty standing in New York Bay, there is inscribed a poem of great beauty by Emma Lazarus. Its words have extended a note of welcome and hope to a vast flow of immigrants that has passed by, many of whom were fleeing oppression in the Old World. The invitation ends, "Send them, the homeless, tempest tossed to me; I lift my lamp beside the golden door."

There had been tempests enough for some of the early comers in the North Atlantic, where they had managed to endure them in wooden sailing vessels. But the worst storms were the ones they had left behind, the winds of religious warfare that had devastated Europe for over a hundred years.

These were the real American pilgrims. We find them identified not only in the poem at the statue, but also in the ancient prophetic writings of Isaiah: "Oh you afflicted, tossed with tempest and not comforted . . . great shall be the peace of your children." And they did find peace, with themselves as well as with their God.

It should not seem strange to us that the Almighty should provide a haven for his church. The Church of Jesus Christ is the most important thing there is in this world, if you believe the Bible. All of history is revolving around her and is rushing toward that destiny that shall see her as coheir of all creation along with Christ, her Lord and Savior.

The Bible tells us a lot about the church, as well as the events, major and minor, which she has experienced during these last two millenniums. Here in chapter 12 of Revelation, we find a miniature perspective of the life of the church through our age. Like the parables of Christ, the truths contained there spill out in a flow of symbolic language that conceals the meaning of the prophecy to those who are just mildly curious. And like any well-coded message, the solution can only be found by engaging in an energetic search into the ways the same symbols are used at other times—in this case, in the rest of the Bible. And that especially includes the Old Testament. I think Christ, the author of Revelation, had that in mind when he said, "Whosoever reads, let him understand" (Matthew 24:15). This kind of prophetic writing takes a lot of reading.

So then, there is mystery involved in this remarkable prophetic chapter, as well as romance and suspense. There is even the appearance of a flesh-eating dragon and a lovely woman in distress. And yet, this in no fairy tale. The characters and events are absolutely true to life.

A WONDER IN HEAVEN

The vision starts at the beginning of our age when the Roman Empire was near its zenith and the kingdom of God was about to suffer a violent change of hands.

> *And there appeared a great wonder in heaven, a woman clothed with the sun and the moon under her feet, and upon her head a crown of twelve stars. And she, being with child, cried, and pained to be delivered.* (Revelation 12:1-2)

The scene opens with a view of things in heaven. It is not the heaven where God's throne is or even the heavens that surround the earth. Rather, it is the kingdom of heaven on earth that John saw, and it has been a battleground between the servants of God and the servants of Satan ever since the days of Moses.

This kingdom of heaven is the worship of the true God in the earth, and it has to do with spiritual things rather than physical. In microcosm, it was there with Abel when he offered the fruit of his flock, and it was also there with Jacob when he dreamed of the ladder to heaven. It became organized when Moses gave the law from God, and it included all Israelites, whether they were spiritually born again or not, as not all Israelites were children of God—nor are they all today. Jesus called some of them children of the devil (John 8:44, Romans 2:28-29).

The kingdom of heaven existed in that strict form through the Old Testament time until the Day of Pentecost, when it assumed the new flavor of the New Testament Church. The Lord Jesus told some Jews that God would be taking the kingdom of heaven away from their nation and giving it to other nations that would be willing to bear its spiritual fruit. Look up Matthew 21:43 for this important piece of information. It was in the context of this larger aspect of the kingdom of heaven that John saw the events begin to unfold that he was to record.

Quickly, the vision narrowed from the church in its largest physical aspect under the Jews to include just the children of God, symbolized by the woman with child. Now here is the core of the church, genuine believers, the elect of God, the bride of the Son of God with all her identifying marks upon her. She has been called the *elect lady* and the Lamb's wife (Revelation 21:9). She appeared to John wearing a garment likened to the sun, which, to us, is the brilliance of the light of God and the "Sun of Righteousness" (Malachi 4:2).

And the moon is under her feet. The moon, as seen here, seems to represent those of earth's people who reflect the light of God—the sun. This is what we do as Christians. We put on Christ, as Ephesians 4 tells us, and we let our lights shine. But the light really comes from God, and we reflect it as the moon reflects the sun. The woman was wearing the sun, but by having the moon under her feet, the symbolism shows us that the church is in authority in the earth, an authority which she also gets from Christ Jesus, her Lord.

Then the twelve stars upon the woman's head is another identifying mark. It takes in not only the roots of the kingdom in the Old Testament under the twelve tribes of Israel, but also carries forward into our own time through the twelve apostles of the Lamb.

If we paraphrase this remarkable first verse, this is what we might have—"And there appeared a great wonder in the transcendent kingdom of God, the church showing forth the light and character of Christ her master, with authority over the saints and heir to the covenant of Abraham and the covenant of grace as delivered to the apostles."

This full introduction of the church was necessary because she will be the main character in this prophetic vision. We are observing her as the Lord Jesus was about to be born. For centuries, the stage was being set for this event, and there were multiplied prophecies waiting to be fulfilled. But before the action can begin, there must be another introduction.

THE RED DRAGON

There was more in the organized kingdom of heaven in that day than just worshippers. There were also some effective impostors who were in positions of power and authority, sitting in Moses's seat (Matthew 23:2-4), and to whom Christ said, "You are of your father the devil." So this next phase of the vision reveals and identifies their father, the devil himself.

> *And there appeared another wonder in heaven, and behold a great red dragon, having seven heads and ten horns, and seven crowns upon his heads. And his tail drew the third part of the stars of heaven, and did cast them to the earth. And the dragon stood before the woman which was ready to be delivered for to devour her child as soon as it was born.* (12:3-4)

The seven heads upon the beast will be seen particularly when we get to chapter 13 of Revelation. They represent seven great world empires over which Satan has successively reigned ever since ancient times.

There is a popular idea that Satan's act of drawing the third part of the stars after him may have reference to his initial fall into sin and a third of the angels of God following him into his rebellion. This passage may indeed have some reference to that, but as far as the context is concerned, it has immediate reference to the religious authorities and leaders of Israel during the time that Christ was upon the earth. Stars are sometimes used in prophecy to mean people of importance and power.

The Bible tells us that some of the Pharisees believed on Jesus, and even some of the members of the Sanhedrin did as well. But enough of them were unbelievers that they were able to muscle their agenda into effect and get the Son of God crucified. It doesn't take a majority to do that, but only a committed minority. As little as the third part of a group can easily control the entire body if they are committed enough.

I have had the experience of seeing it happen in churches on more than one occasion. The communists who controlled the Soviet Empire were never in the majority, but they still had their way. Satan knew that the Messiah was about to be born, and a prophecy in Zechariah 3 tells us that he was prepared to resist him with all his power. His first act was to influence King Herod to attempt to kill him. Later, after Jesus's ministry began, the effort to kill him increased until Christ's Crucifixion, at last, accomplished what Satan wanted to do.

> *And she brought forth a man child who was to rule all nations with a rod of iron, and her child was caught up unto God and to His throne.* (12:5)

Not only is the birth of Christ pictured here in this woman's deliverance, but his death and resurrection as well. He had warned his disciples shortly before he went to the cross, "A woman when she is in travail has sorrow because her hour is come and you now therefore have sorrow. But I will see you again, and your heart shall rejoice" (John 16:21-22). And so his hour came as he completed his earthly mission, and he did see his disciples again, as he said, before he ascended back to the throne of his Father. He is seated there, as Psalm 110:1 says, waiting until the time when his Father makes his enemies his footstool.

FLIGHT INTO THE WILDERNESS

> *And the woman fled into the wilderness, where she has a place prepared of God, that they should feed her there a thousand two hundred and threescore days.* (12:6)

Soon after the Lord Jesus returned to the Father, the fledgling church—the woman—began to come under terrific persecution, first from the Jewish authorities and then from the Roman Empire. These hard times were not outside the plans and purposes of God, of course. In fact, Christ had warned his disciples by quoting a line from the Old Testament, "I will smite the shepherd, and the sheep shall be scattered" (Mark 14:27). But one of the effects of the persecution, as shown in Acts 8:4, was to spread the Gospel faster and farther.

The persecutions became so intense that the church had to learn to operate in an underground mode. The caves underneath the city of Rome were used by Christians for meetings and for burial places. In other countries, they met where they could—in secluded rooms or out in the open in the forests and fields. The church truly fled to the wilderness, and the true element of the church had to remain there for many hundreds of years until the Protestant Reformation made it safer—at least in parts of Northern Europe—to come out again.

Some will say that such an underground church never existed. They didn't keep many records because record keeping was dangerous. However, the fact that the Roman Catholic Church had to wage a constant battle against loosely organized heretics is just a small part of the evidence that another church was alive during these centuries besides the one that gave its full allegiance to the empire and the Romish church.

WAR IN HEAVEN

The Apostle Paul wrote to the Ephesian Church, and to us as well, "For we wrestle not against flesh and blood, but against principalities, against powers, against rulers of the darkness of this world, against spiritual wickedness in high places" (Ephesians 6:12). When the Reformation finally came, in the 1500s, the battle was not just among Catholics and dissenters, or the emperor and his princes, but it was between good and bad principles and good angels and fallen angels as well. Paul wrote about these battles, "For the weapons of our warfare are not carnal, but mighty through God to the pulling down of strongholds" (2 Corinthians 10:4). So here is Revelation's description of the Protestant Reformation:

> *And there was war in heaven. Michael and his angels fought against the dragon, and the dragon fought and his angels, and prevailed not; neither was their place found anymore in heaven.* (12:7-8)

Thus, the church of Jesus Christ, which is the kingdom of heaven in the earth, became engulfed with violence for more than a hundred years after Martin Luther began his confrontation with the Catholic Church over its offenses. All across Europe, pulpits began to blaze away with the artillery of free grace as men began to learn, as Luther did, that the just live by their faith, and not by penance, confessions to priests, and the paying of indulgences.

> *And the great red dragon was cast out, that old serpent, called the devil, and Satan, who deceives the whole world. He was cast out into the earth, and his angels were cast out with him.* (12:9)

The Roman Church and the empire fought back, of course, with a mighty effort that we call the Counter-Reformation. Such was their success that huge portions of Europe that had fallen away from their church were restored, largely through the work and leadership of the Jesuit Order. All of Southern Europe was regained so that, even today, there is a marked contrast between the religious atmosphere of Southern and Northern Europe.

The casting out of Satan from heaven to the earth has to be taken symbolically. Heaven is the church in this sense; therefore, at this time a major part of the church was freed from the controlling presence of Satan. The earth into which he went may mean actually that Satan, after the upheaval of the Reformation had passed, moved his chief base of operations out of the church that he had joined several centuries before, back to his usual haunts of secular power—the capitals of the world. Historically, this happened. The Holy Roman Empire that had backed the Roman Church with all its formidable might continued its decline until, by the year 1648, it lost its power to rule over the emerging countries of Europe.

> *And I heard a loud voice saying in heaven, now is come salvation and strength, and the kingdom of our God, and the power of His Christ. For the accuser of our brethren is cast down, which accused them before our God day and night. And they overcame him by the blood of the Lamb, and by the word of their testimony, and they loved not their lives unto the death.* (12:10-11)

This exclamation of praise and thanksgiving is made to God for his deliverance of the churches of Northern Europe from 1,260 years of bondage, much like the Israelites singing and praising on the shores of the Red Sea after their deliverance from Egypt's bondage. Actually, the Reformation was more than a religious battle. It was also social and economic and included many small wars such as the Peasants' Revolt in Germany. It has been described as the terrible scream of oppressed humanity.

> *Therefore rejoice you heavens, and you who dwell in them. Woe to the inhabitants of the earth and the sea! For the devil is come down unto you, having great wrath, because he knows that he has but a short time.* (12:12)

The world is now in this short time of which Satan is aware. Obviously, he is going to be trying harder when he knows his time is giving out. Perhaps that is a reason why so much bloodshed has occurred during the twentieth century with its world wars. Satan does not know all things as God does, but he does know there will be an end to his attempt to reign sovereignly on this earth.

> *And when the dragon saw that he was cast out into the earth, he persecuted the woman which brought forth the man child.* (12:13)

Within the short span of fifty years, the Reformation had swept over much of Europe, severely limiting both the pope's and the emperor's stranglehold on the continent. The reaction to this was swift. Under the brilliant leadership of the Jesuits, the kings of Southern Europe fielded their armies against the rebellious provinces, and there followed a hundred years of war.

But persecution of dissenters had been firmly ingrained into the Christian religion in Europe. Even some of the reformed groups, such as the Church of England, felt it was their responsibility to make sure everybody kept exactly the same faith as that was held by the men in charge.

So they produced even more martyrs to add to the long lists of those who had been killed by the Roman Empire and the Holy Roman Empire. Obviously, there needed to be more deliverance even after the Reformation had done its work.

ON EAGLES' WINGS

> *And to the woman were given two wings of a great eagle, that she might fly into the wilderness, into her place, where she is nourished for a time, and times, and half a time, from the face of the serpent.* (12:14)

So here is the second time the woman had to fly away to a wilderness. The wilderness into which she had initially fled (verse 6) had, by now, become full of civilized nations. Where was there another one into which to flee? There was yet another, a vast newly discovered continent that had been waiting for thousands of years to become a safe haven for oppressed Christians.

Only eight years after the last martyr died in England, the first congregation of pilgrims touched ground at Plymouth Rock in what was to become the state of Massachusetts. Others followed fast behind them as on eagle's wings they came to fulfill this great prophecy—and also the lines in Isaiah 40:31: "But they that wait upon the Lord shall renew their strength. They shall mount up on wings as eagles."

From France alone in the year 1685, about five hundred thousand Huguenots (French Protestants) fled away from their homeland, and many came to America. It is not surprising, therefore, that the United States should have chosen the eagle as her national symbol. No doubt it was God's choice.

How long shall this haven last? How long is a time, times, and half a time? This expression, found also in Daniel, seems to imply, by its very language, that it is a time of unknown duration. But it also implies exactness, and in God's mind, it will last until the moment he purposes to end it.

> *And the serpent cast out of his mouth water as a flood after the woman, that he might cause her to be carried away of the flood. And the earth helped the woman, and the earth opened her mouth and swallowed up the flood which the dragon cast out of his mouth.* (12:15-16)

The flood that was cast after the American pilgrims was a flood of armed might. This symbol is used frequently in prophecy to represent military invasions. Isaiah 8:7 is one scripture among many. And the armies and navies did come—the British during the Revolutionary War and the Japanese and Germans in recent world wars.

What was the thing that swallowed up these forces of aggression? It was the immense size of the two oceans that God had placed on either side of our continent. Until today, no invader has been able to successfully wage war across them. The very size of the earth was the thing that provided the barrier that saved us until our forces could be built and marshaled for defense.

Today, these oceans are not the barrier they once were. Intercontinental ballistic missiles and nuclear warheads have changed the picture greatly. But at the same time, we in America have accumulated the might to stand up to aggression from wherever it may come.

For America, the story ends at this point. This may mean that there will be no more aggression against our shores—or it may mean that if there is any, that the earth in some way will again swallow it up. All this also seems to mean that America will be a meaningful, safe haven for the true, liberated church until man's history comes to the end and Christ comes back. After all, it is the church that God is protecting, not just a geographical area of the world.

> *And the dragon was wrathful with the woman and went to make war with the remnant of her seed, which keep the commandments of God and have the testimony of Jesus Christ.* (12:17)

A very significant point that has been made in this prophecy is that when the woman fled the second time (to America), the devil was not allowed to follow her. Apparently, Satan's base of operations, after being thrown out of the church, had to stay in the Old World from which point he could only cast his waves of wrath against the protected church.

But there was something else he could do. He could make war with the remnant of the church's seed that were left in Europe, as verse 17 tells us. And this has happened severely. Adolf Hitler persecuted Jews, and many countries of the Old World have done it as well, though not as severely. Some of the worst of the oppression, however, was that which the communist revolution caused against Christian believers in Russia as well as in the far-flung parts of the communist empire.

The dragon is now in these days taking his last stand. He knows that the last trumpet is about to sound and that his empire will be demolished. The kingdoms of this world are about to "become the kingdoms of our Lord and of His Christ, and He shall reign for ever and ever."

Chapter 17

The Beast

After showing to us first the fortunes of the Bible and then the fortunes of the church, the third special feature of Revelation will reveal to us the fortunes of world government. Here, John, like Daniel, stands upon the shore of the sea and sees a strange animal-like creature in vision rising out of the sea.

> *And I stood upon the sand of the sea, and saw a beast rise up out of the sea, having seven heads and ten horns, and upon his horns ten crowns, and upon his heads the name of blasphemy. And the beast which I saw was like unto a leopard, and his feet were as the feet of a bear, and his mouth as the mouth of a lion; and the dragon gave him his power and his seat and great authority.* (Revelation 13:1-2)

This beast, or animal form, is shown to have several revealing characteristics. It has the names of blasphemy upon its head, so we can see immediately that this creature is against God and his kingdom. It received its great power from the dragon, who is Satan, and it has great authority. The statement about authority gives us a clue about his identity. It matches up with the words of Satan that were spoken to Christ on the mount of temptation. On that occasion, Satan was showing him a vision of all the nations of the world and said, "All this power I will give you, and the glory of them, for that is delivered unto me, and to whomsoever I will I give it" (Luke 4:6). Satan, of course, is a liar, but was he lying when he said these words? It's unlikely that he would do that, knowing that Jesus would know that it was a lie. He absolutely does have power over the nations to raise up rulers and governments—but always within the permission of God.

So here we have in this seven-headed beast, what many Bible expositors have agreed, is a display in vivid form of all the world empires that been formed through the history of man. You will remember the world empires that were displayed in Daniel, chapter 2, and they are included among these seven. Daniel's prophecy began at the time of the Babylonian Empire. This vision in Revelation 13 begins before that, at the very beginning of the empires of man.

There were two mighty empires that existed before Nebuchadnezzar's time, and they had successively held authority over most of the known world. The first of these very earliest empires was the kingdom and empire of Egypt, and the second was the empire of the Assyrians. Egypt, as we know from the Book of Exodus, held the people of Israel in slavery, and Assyria was the nation that destroyed the northern kingdom of Israel during the days of the kings (2 Kings 17).

If we count up all the world empires that played these prominent parts in Bible history and world events, we find that they come to seven. They are the following: (1) Egypt, (2) Assyria, (3) Babylon, (4) Persia, (5) Greece, (6) Rome, and (7) Colonial Europe. All these make up the seven heads upon this awesome beast that John saw and which had such great authority.

The rest of chapter 13 gives us much additional information for understanding the identity and function of the beast. The head that existed in John's day was the sixth one, which represented the Roman Empire in all its glory. The prophetic narrative picks up there with the age of Rome in verse 3 and shows what would be happening in the future from John's time onward:

> *And I saw one of its heads as it were wounded to death; and his deadly wound was healed: and all the world wondered after the beast.*

In the year AD 395, the Roman Empire broke into two parts—the Eastern Empire with its capital in Constantinople and the Western part with its capital in Rome. Christ Jesus has said that a house divided against itself cannot stand; therefore, this division of the Roman Empire should have been a mortal wound.

However, such was the power and dream of empire that was still in the hearts of men that the empire of Rome was miraculously revived. In the year AD 800, Charlemagne was declared to be the new emperor, and Roman imperialism was allowed to continue. It continued to live for a much longer time under the modified name of Holy Roman Empire. It finally came to its end about 1650.

> *And there was given to him a mouth speaking great things and blasphemies; and power was given unto him to continue forty and two months.*

Verse 5 tells us that this head, which was Rome, would continue to live for 42 months. Given 30 days to a month, the 42 months would amount to 1,260 days. If we again apply this number to years instead of days, we would find that after the healing of its wounded head, Rome would continue to live for 1,260 years. We know that the deadly wound occurred in AD 395. Therefore, adding the 1,260 years to that date would bring us to the year 1655. This was a very important time in the life of the Holy Roman Empire and the emerging countries of Europe.

The Treaty of Westphalia, which spelled the end of the Holy Roman Emperor's accepted authority, was made in the year 1648. However, travel was slow in those days, and the king of England did not manage to sign it until two years later—in 1650. By the time word got around and the provisions of the treaty began to be implemented, the year 1655 was probably the date that was on everyone's calendar.

What a remarkable prophecy—God telling us that the Roman Empire would sustain a deadly wound in AD 395, would be revived and continue for 1,260 years. And exactly 1,260 years later, the history books tell us that withering empire lost its universal control that had marked it out as a world-class empire for so long!

> *And it was given him to make war with the saints, and to overcome them: and power was given him over all kindreds, and tongues, and nations.* (Verse 7)

Here we see the Roman Empire going about its infamous war against Christians. The persecutions started early, even recorded in the Book of Acts, and continued through the Dark Ages and Middle Ages. The Holy Roman Empire was supposedly a Christian government, but in reality, it was not. In the Book of Revelation, God gives us two unique code expressions to help us identify the people of God and the people of Satan, and these codes appear several times in the course of the prophecy. Here the Christians are called *kindreds, tongues, and nations,* an expression that first appears in chapter 7, verse 9 and which is clearly identified there as the church. The other code phrase is this:

> *And all that dwell upon the earth shall worship him, whose names are not written in the Book of Life of the Lamb slain from the foundation of the world.* (Verse 8)

Those whom Christ called the children of the devil (John 8:44) are frequently warring against the born-again people of God. They are simply dwelling on the earth, and they do it as if they own it. But they do not. Jesus said that the meek are blessed because they shall inherit the earth (Matthew 5:5). This earth belongs to us, and we will inherit it fully when our Lord comes back again (Daniel 7:27) although, in the meantime, we are often persecuted by the others who are simply dwelling upon it. We, the saints, have our names written in the Book of Life, and they have been recorded there since before the world began, as this verse says. Ephesians 1:4 verifies that. Now this picture of persecution continues.

THE IMAGE TO THE BEAST

> *And I beheld another beast coming up out of the earth; and he had two horns like a lamb, and he spoke as a dragon. And he exercised all the power of the first beast before him, and caused the earth and those who dwell therein to worship the first beast, whose deadly wound was healed.* (Verses 11-12)

Here we have vividly described the unholy marriage between the Roman Catholic popes and the emperors of the empire. The popes were recognized as the ecclesiastical power of the empire and the emperors as the secular power. In reality, they overlapped and, for many hundreds of years, vied with each other for power. Their common purpose was agreed upon, which was to stamp out all opposition to the empire and the Roman Church. This they did remarkably well, and persecution of dissenting Christian groups waged on for the whole 1,260 years that the beast reigned—and even continues to this day in some Catholic-dominated countries.

It is not our purpose here to record many of the details of this reign of the empire and the Roman Church through this long span of time. A good work for briefly referencing this subject is *Halley's Bible Handbook*. It has an excellent handy history about these times in the back section under "Church History."

> *And he deceived those who dwell on the earth by means of those miracles which he had power to do in the sight of the beast; saying to them who dwell on the earth, that they should make an image to the beast, which had a wound by a sword, and did live ... and cause that as many as would not worship the beast should be killed.* (Verses 14-15b)

This image to the beast of empire was—and still is today—the office, outward image, and regalia of the popes of Rome. It's all there, from the elaborate throne, the sedan chair, and the untold treasures of wealth to the authoritative rule that is exercised. It is generally patterned after what the Roman emperors were and what they had. And who is it that is deceived by all this? "Those who dwell on the earth," who are not of the Lord Jesus Christ.

Now this does not mean that all Catholic Christians are going to hell. Not by any means. Many Catholics are part of that church simply because they were born into it or found some solace or meaning in it—but are no more aware of the deeper meaning of it all than many Protestants are aware of what their churches and denominations stand for.

> *And he caused all, both small and great, rich and poor, free and bond, to receive a mark in their right hand, or in their foreheads. And that no man might buy and sell, except he who had the mark, or the name of the beast, or the number of his name.* (Verses 16-17)

It is no longer the practice in most Catholic countries today, but the policy of the Roman Church in the Middle Ages was that no one would be allowed to operate business and work without expressing allegiance to the Catholic system and taking its mark. Even today, in the strictest Catholic countries (such as in some of the states of Mexico), it is hard for Protestants to live normally. During the Middle Ages, it was even simpler. Non-Catholics were sometimes simply executed or run out of the country. And Catholics were not the only Christians who did these things. The Church of England had its part in persecutions as well. We can thank the Lord that things do change and improve. Today, no Christian denominations execute those who are dissenters to their beliefs and practices. And today, there are many good Catholic churches, pastors, and members. Would to God that were true of all religions. It is not. Even today, Christians are sometimes killed in the name of Allah in Muslim countries.

The mark of the beast could be any mark it chooses during the long reign of power of these seven world empires. During the Roman Catholic reign, it has been the cross more than anything else. Loraine Boettner, in his book *Roman Catholicism*, treats on the way in which the cross was first used by the Emperor Constantine as a sign under which to wage warfare and also how it has long been used as the identifying mark for recognized Catholics, being traced on their hands and foreheads during ceremonies of dedication. It is significant that Christian groups that are of Baptist heritage have traditionally refused to use the cross as a symbol of their belief. This can be observed in the older Baptist church buildings, which never used crosses as decoration. Baptists have begun to use crosses on the buildings only in recent times.

Chapter 18

Evangelism and Reformation

Chapter 13 has presented to us a dramatic prophetic exposé of Satan's successful efforts to rule over as much of the earth as he can through the use of world empires and powerful churches. In chapter 12, we saw the end of Satan's monopoly of domination and the deliverance that came blazing through with the advent of the Protestant Reformation. Now as we come to chapter 14, the scene is set for more world evangelism and reformation by God's *kindreds, tongues, and peoples.*

Chapter 14 shows to us harpers busy at their praise music and new songs being sung that anticipated a new age in the earth. And so it has been with the dawn of the Age of Enlightenment that came after the Reformation, together with the new freedom of worship, has ushered in our modern age as we know it and an ongoing spread of religious freedom.

Verse 6 graphically describes the Gospel going forth into new regions, as has been the case these last several hundred years. A sickle is thrust into the earth, and God begins a new and expanded reaping of saints into his earthly kingdom. This was indeed what transpired when the Reformation took hold of the peoples of Northern Europe and spread to America. Then there came the world evangelism movement that was birthed in the 1800s and carried the Gospel to many regions that had not received it before. And then more lately came the praise and worship movement that began mostly in the 1960s and has now spread worldwide and is still going on full force.

Chapters 15 and 16 tell us about God's last plagues that would be sent upon the earth. These vials, or bowls of wrath, are no doubt symbolic in nature, as much of the rest of Revelation is. In verse 10 of chapter 16, the darkness that was sent upon the seat of the beast may have reference to the Dark Ages that resulted from the corruption that had settled upon the church and government.

In verse 12, there is pictured the drying up of the symbolic river that is the dividing line between East and West. This did occur during our twentieth century as Western powers engaged Far Eastern powers in warfare for the first time on a global scale. This thrusts us into the last age of time, and the scene is now set for last things to happen.

END-TIME SPIRITUAL OPPRESSION

> *And I saw three unclean spirits like frogs come out of the mouth of the dragon, and out of the mouth of the beast, and out of the mouth of the false prophet. For they are the spirits of devils, working miracles, which go forth unto the kings of the earth and of the whole world, to gather them to the battle of that great day of God Almighty.* (Revelation 16:13-14)

This scripture seems to have to do with the pouring out of the sixth vial or bowl of wrath. I have always been somewhat mystified by this chapter in Revelation, but I do have the conviction that these progressive outpourings of the wrath of God have been interspersed at points throughout this age of the church that we have been living through. My general feeling is that they have a lot to do with warfare between good and bad spirits. We do know that this real warfare is ongoing all around us, as numerous scriptures verify. The author, Frank Peretti, has brought this out in his remarkable novels. Needless to say, devils or demons do exist. There is ample warning about them in the New Testament. We sometimes prefer to ignore them, of course, but there are times when we simply need to know what it is that they are up to.

The Bible tells us plainly not to worship idols, but it is not an idol of stone or wood that is the danger. Why is there such a conflict between the worship of idols and the worship of the true God? It is because there is present, in connection with each idol, a living demon. The demon's presence is there to claim the worship and attention that the idol is receiving, and he works through this process of worship and devotion to create satanic strongholds in the minds of worshippers and to control and manipulate people. You should read about this in 2 Timothy 2:24-26, etc. Is that really true? Does the Bible actually tell us that the worshipping of idols is the same as worshipping devils? Yes, indeed.

The Apostle Paul wrote in 1 Corinthians 10:20, "But I say that the things which the Gentiles sacrifice, they sacrifice to devils, and not to God; and I would not that you should have fellowship with devils."

So it has to be one or the other—God or demons—and the conflict inevitably comes. In this Revelation passage above, we see an increase of demonic activity in the last times. Actual unclean spirits are seen being released into the world to do their work. And it says that the source of the first flow of evil spirits is from the mouth of *Satan himself*. He is the dragon in this passage of scripture. That is explained in Revelation 12:9.

This increase in demonic presence and activity from the very person of Satan would account for the huge rise of interest, and that has occurred in recent times in occult activity and even in the direct worship of Satan. The Church of Satan, for example, is now flourishing in some places.

Much of the occult influence in our culture today, however, does not connect directly with Satan, but rather indirectly. For example, in the little avant-garde shopping district not far from my office here in Macon, Georgia (in the center of the U.S. "Bible belt"), there have been three New Age shops opened in recent months. New Age teaching—which is abounding in America and the rest of the Western World—functions like a cleverly disguised trap. It draws unsuspecting, curious, and often unhappy people into a web of great-sounding, exotic dogma that promises all sorts of improvements in their lives.

This is a melding of some Christian thought with Eastern religions and includes the idea that all religions lead to the same place—which is a higher life through meditation and contact with spirit guides—and eventual arrival at a high plane of perfection through successive experiences of reincarnation. The New Age Movement, which tried to bring in an occult revolution in the 1970s, failed to do so, and since then, we have heard less about it. But Satan's occult work is still abounding today in more conventional and "respectable" ways.

In the Revelation scripture above, we observe that the next flow of demons is out of the beast. This beast is the symbol that is used in Revelation to describe Satan's seeking of dominion for himself through empire building. But he is much more than that. He is a demon individual himself, probably of very high position, no doubt next to Satan himself—and he is Satan's chief general and governmental organizer.

We know he is a demon because he is seen being cast into the lake of fire later in Revelation.

The fresh demonic flow out of this demon's mouth in recent times has brought about the great frenzied efforts that are being mounted to institute a new world government. That's nothing new, actually, when we consider the march of fanatical men through time who have aspired, and sometimes succeeded, in conquering all the known civilized worlds in their time, thus making world empires.

Within the lifetime of many people still living, this "beast" has been seen successively working through German Nazism, also the worldwide communist revolution, as well as other more minor efforts to rule the world. Today the main thrust of this effort is through the United Nations. This, by the way, is also a core part of the New Age Movement, and it has the favor and backing of key people and groups all over the world. It is, no doubt, Satan's hope that he can pull this one off before Christ Jesus returns and installs his own worldwide millennial kingdom. We will then definitely get a world government, but it will be under King Jesus Christ.

The third source of evil forces is out of the mouth of *the false prophet*. This also is a high-level demon (who also is cast into the lake of fire later), and he is in charge of infiltrating the church of Jesus Christ, taking control wherever he can, and either destroying or capturing as much of the flock of God as he can.

One place he is seen today is in the very powerful movement of *liberal Christianity*, which has literally exploded in the Christian community during the last several decades. This great unclean spirit works through human beings, of course, as they all do. The human counterparts to the false prophet are clearly described in 1 John 2, 2 John, and Jude.

There are indeed false prophets in the church. They deceive a lot of Christians because *they look good, sound good, and even do a little good*. They are sometimes the biggest workers for humanitarian projects. But they fail to pass the acid identity test of a true prophet, which is in 1 John 2:22: "Who is a liar but he that denies that Jesus is the Christ?" They deny (if they are pressed to admit it) miracles of the Bible, the virgin birth, the biblical definition of sin, the substitutionary sacrifice of Christ on the cross, and the real biblical meaning of blood redemption.

The awful reality is that much of the Christian community in America today has been under the spell of this flood of unclean spirits that is proceeding out of the mouth of the great false prophet of Satan's empire.

The victims of these false prophets may be children of God, or they may not be. Even the "elect" can be temporarily fooled—though not permanently (Matthew 24:24). After this account of three great demonic spirits and their end-time destructive powers, the next phrase reads,

Behold, I come quickly. Blessed is he that watches, and keeps his garments, lest he walk naked and they see his shame.

But what about this great flood of destructive spirits that is being released upon the earth? As far as Satan's fate is concerned, he will be captured and bound up by a strong angel when Christ makes his return (Revelation 20). That's the premillennial view. If you are "amil," he still comes to an end and is cast into the lake of fire.

What happens to the other two great spirits—the beast and the false prophet—is interesting. In Revelation 19:20, we have seen them being captured and cast into the lake of fire, apparently previous to the time when Satan will be put there. Somehow, the more I read these prophecies, the more I am inclined to see them as not happening all on one day, but rather over a period of time—whether short or long is presently difficult to tell as these events are likely so close at hand.

Could it be that these two evil spirits may have already recently been cast into the lake of fire? Could this removal of the beast from the world scene be the reason for the sudden demise of the Communist Revolutionary Front and the relative peaceful condition of world politics today? Time will tell.

On the other hand, if we yet have another major effort at world conquest to arise in the world, we will know that the beast is still alive and well. We should keep in mind that the purpose of our having biblical prophecies is to help us interpret the present scene within God's plans and purposes and to see how God's foretold work has transpired in the past—and is not for predicting the future.

Then if the false prophet also has been removed, that might account for the resurgence of conservative biblical Christianity that has been taking place and the exposing of some Christian leaders who basically discount the Bible as being factual. So is God now bringing his true church into position for some victories in preparation for Christ's return?

We just need to keep strongly in mind the words quoted above about keeping our righteous garments and watching. These are exciting times. Then we notice Revelation 16:16.

> *And he gathered them together into a place called in the Hebrew tongue Armageddon.*

So Jesus is coming soon, and we are to be ready to meet him. I believe a last war is coming soon although I also think that the word *Armageddon* probably applies to all the wars of this past twentieth century. There is something significant about that name. It comes from the plain of Megiddo, and that is the place where good King Josiah of Judah tried to play the policeman by preventing the king of Egypt from sending his expeditionary force against the king of Babylon (2 Chronicles 35).

It is significant that this is the same philosophy held today, that no nation will be allowed to war against another even if God sends it. That is UN policy and has come to be an American policy. Meanwhile, the lessons of scripture go unheeded, no one being aware that God actually sent the king of Egypt against Babylon on that occasion and also that King Josiah got himself killed when he tried to interfere. Perhaps that same secular, godless policy will lead us yet into another great war, which may be the last of all.

Will there be a nuclear war? History says probably so. Man has always used his most ultimate machines of war either to gain something he wants or to defend himself. Bible prophecy seems to indicate that a last war is coming. Even some recent prophecies seem to call out for it. Here is one that was given in 1997: "Listen across the spaces and hear the sound of marching armies. They are coming to do My will, for I have sent them and they are Mine. For there will be destruction and sorrow, but I shall have joy in My house. For you are to gather My people—the ones who have made a covenant with Me by sacrifice, and they shall stand firm in the day of destruction and loss, for they are faithful, and they bear My name, and they are holy."

This may be a single war or a series of wars that occur like repeated charges of a battering ram against a fortress. It may be that the "just" wars of the last century have already been either a part of this war or may be preludes to it.

MORE ABOUT THE BEAST

The story about Rome is not yet over in John's Revelation. The beast of world empire pops up again in chapter 17, this time still under its sixth head, which was Rome. There it is pictured for us in a unique way. It is supporting and carrying a woman who is a harlot. What does this mean? Throughout the Bible, harlotry is symbolic of idolatrous worship. It is the act of perverting the worship of the true and living God.

The symbol of harlotry was used frequently in the writings of the Old Testament prophets in reference to Israel's constant idolatries and the awful judgments that were brought upon them by God because of it. Just as the beast of empire was seen carrying the harlot, as a rule the empires of this world have supported such idolatrous worship, which often was compulsory on the pain of death. And because the worship of God and devils does not mix, they have also persecuted the people of God. Daniel and his friends experienced this problem firsthand in the fiery furnace and the lion's den.

And now, in chapter 17, we see the Roman Empire with the same agenda on its mind. The Christians who were martyred in the Roman coliseum were not just hated because they were different. They were hated and killed because their beliefs were in direct opposition to practices of worship of the Romans.

> *And I saw the woman drunken with the blood of the saints, and with the blood of the martyrs of Jesus; and when I saw her I wondered with great astonishment.* (17:6)

The beast that was carrying the harlot is further identified as Rome in verse 9, where she is shown sitting upon seven mountains. Rome is, of course, the city upon seven hills. This does not mean that the entire beast is Roman. Keep in mind that the beast only operates under one head at a time, and this was just the time that belonged to Rome. Verse 10 shows this to be true:

> *And there are seven kings: five are fallen, and one is, and the other is not yet come; and when he comes he must continue a short space.*

These kings in this vision are not individual men, but rather are whole governments belonging to the great empires through time. Surely enough, five had already fallen by the time the Romans had come along. The fallen ones were Egypt, Assyria, Babylon, Persia, and Greece. Then the scripture says, "One is." That one was the Roman Empire in John's time. Then after that, there would be one more to come, and only one.

This statement agrees with the dream image of Daniel 2 that we saw earlier. There was only one more division in Nebuchadnezzar's dream image after the Roman Empire. Europe during the colonial period would be the last head upon the beast.

At this point, a very interesting technicality arises. There are only seven heads upon the beast, and yet, verse 11 speaks about an eighth one:

> *And the beast that was, and is not, even he is the eighth, and is of the seven, and goes into perdition.*

The "was and is not and yet is" angle is just that these empires keep cropping up only to fall as another takes its place. Satan never gives up, then God comes along, tears up his playhouse, and he has to start over again. The statement about an eighth head is mysterious because the scriptures show there to be only seven heads upon the beast of world empire. But as the last legitimate head was finished as colonialism died with World War II, Satan tried again, quickly this time, because he knows his time is short. The new communist empire, led by the Soviet Union, wasted no time in getting started as the war ended. Eventually, it took in Russia, many countries of Eastern Europe, China, Southeast Asia, and some other small countries. Some are still communist today, such as Vietnam and Cuba, but their power is gone. Then strangely, the whole effort at another world empire disintegrated in about 1990, ending even more suddenly than it started. Today (2010) the Islamic powers seem to be trying to take over the world. But there will be no eighth head upon the beast. Count on it.

> *And the ten horns which you saw are ten kings, which have received no kingdom as yet: but receive power as kings one hour with the beast.* (17:12)

Here we have the nations of Europe not yet arising out of the Roman Empire. Ten is the number of Europe. Remember that in Daniel 2, there was scriptural emphasis placed upon the fact that there were ten toes upon the iron and clay feet of Nebuchadnezzar's image. This, then, is the Europe that existed after Rome, when each nation began to seek its own welfare, independence, and expansion.

Why is Europe's number 10? Generally, through recent centuries, ten nations have in fact made up the core and substance of Europe. More exactly, language, which largely determines the lines where national borders are drawn, has specified Europe's number as being ten. Ever since the episode at the Tower of Babel, differences in language have been the cause of the chief separations between nations. Study shows that there are exactly ten root languages among the European people.

So according to this prophecy, these ten nations were to rule for one hour with the beast. In other words, the countries of Europe would be the conquering and ruling power in the world for a period of one hour, carrying on the aim and tradition of the Roman Empire and all the other empires before them. The only difference would be that the clay of nationalism would prevent them from uniting under one common government. This is what the prophecy in Daniel 2 had stated.

CHAPTER 19

One Hour with the Beast

At this point, we need to find the meaning of the "one hour" during which the ten nations would be chasing their dreams of empire. Here we see God using a period of time, which obviously cannot be actual. It helps us to know that much. So what do we have? The period of time is in prophetic code, and one hour is the symbol. We have a period of time that has characteristics that are similar to the real period that we are searching for.

> *And the ten horns which you saw are ten kings, which have received no kingdom as yet, but receive power as kings one hour with the beast. These have one mind, and shall give their power and strength to the beast.* (17:12-13)

The most obvious place to begin our search would be to compare the one hour with a larger period of time. OK, a whole day is no doubt the most basic division of time that we have. Next we observe that an hour is the twenty-fourth part of a day. Perhaps God is telling us that the period of time through which the colonial powers of Europe would be reigning would be the *twenty-fourth part* of a much larger day or span of time.

The word *day* in scripture has a variety of uses. God sometimes said, "In that day," and by that he meant a certain era of time, not a twenty-four-hour period. Now it is apparent that the space of time we are looking for is quite large, so let's use the largest possible day that we can find. That would naturally be the day of the whole history of man.

There has been a tradition, both Christian and Hebrew, that goes at least back to the time of the apostles, which states that the world will stand for 6,000 years, and then there will be a thousand-year period of rest. This would be like a Sabbath or rest on the seventh day. From the Christian perspective, that last thousand-year period (the seventh) will be the millennial reign of

Christ upon the earth. Since we are now living at a point about 6,000 years after the creation of Adam, that would possibly mean that the coming of Christ is very near to us at this time. Therefore, if all of human history finally ends up as being a total of 7,000 years, then we could call that the day of man. In that case, the *twenty-fourth part* of such a day would be *291.666 years*. This is an interesting number with an interesting remainder. Actually, this remainder of six goes on for infinity. Also, it is significant that the number *666* is the number of the beast (Revelation 13:18), as if God is putting a tag on this number for us just to show that we are on the right track. One thing that the number of the beast says about Satan is that he never comes out even. He tries to make it to a seven, which is the Bible's number of wholeness, but he only arrives at a 666 with a remainder that goes on forever. He is always imitating God, but forever falls short.

So we have, then, a period of *291* years as the one hour of the great day of man—that the ten governments in Europe would spend with the beast. As we saw earlier, the year *1648* marked the final end of the sixth head upon the beast, which was Rome as it had evolved into the Holy Roman Empire. That was the year of the famous Treaty of Westphalia that recognized the rights of the princes of Europe to exert authority that had previously belonged to the emperor.

Adding 291 forward from that year 1648, we come to the year 1939, which we know to be the year in which World War II began. Is that fact significant? Yes, it is because that big war spelled the death knell of the colonial era. After the war ended in 1945, the whole world got very interested in stopping all further expansion and wars. The United Nations was quickly built as a monument to that principle. The thought of another war with full nuclear confrontation between nations was simply unthinkable. Colonialism had to go. Its day was over.

After verse 12, we are given some added information about the rule of these ten governments with the beast of world empire. During the time of the worldwide colonial power struggle, the iron of the Roman dream of conquest continued with full influence among the ten divisions of Europe:

> *These have one mind, and shall give their power and strength to the beast.* (17:13)

They all had a mind to conquer and expand into the new parts of the world, and they had the strength to do it. Next, we are given a glimpse into how this state of affairs developed. The Holy Roman power did not collapse without a fierce struggle:

> *These shall make war with the Lamb, and the Lamb shall overcome them: for He is Lord of lords, and King of kings: and they that are with Him are called, and chosen, and faithful.* (17:14)

The Protestant Reformation that came in the sixteenth century plunged Europe into a period of war that lasted for a hundred years. It was more than a religious struggle; it was social and economic as well. But religion was key to it all. The oppression of the old feudal system had worked hand in hand with religious oppression that had been just as severe. Needless to say, the Lamb won the struggle as the verse above states, and the wave of Protestant zeal that grew out of the Reformation conflict provided the energy that it took to build the modern nations of Northern Europe and the New World.

When the dust of battle settled, there was much work to be done. God once again had a controversy with the nations, and the harlot that had been riding upon the beast of empire was due for a confrontation.

> *And the ten horns which you saw upon the beast, these shall hate the whore, and shall make her desolate and naked, and shall eat her flesh, and burn her with fire. For God has put it in their hearts to fulfill His will, and to agree, and give their kingdom unto the beast, until the words of God shall be fulfilled.* (17:16-17)

Wherever the European explorers, conquerors, and settlers went, the Gospel of Jesus Christ went with them. The idols of worship that belonged to the people of the newly colonized lands were toppled from their pedestals and broken, like the statue of Dagon before the Ark of the Covenant.

So there we have it. The one hour of time that the nations of Europe would spend with the beast of empire has now ended. There are still some colonial possessions in parts of the world, but the era is very much over. I have made many ministry trips to African countries and have seen how glad the African people are that the colonial settlers have mostly gone home.

BABYLON IS FALLEN

The next chapter in Revelation (18) concerns the destruction of mystic Babylon. What does God mean by this symbol? Some writers have shown it to mean the old Roman Catholic Church. But Mystery Babylon is far more than that. In chapter 17, she was seen riding upon the beast with seven heads, and it therefore follows that this symbol applies in some way to all the great empires that the Bible enumerates for us from Egypt to colonial Europe.

She was pictured in 17:6 as being drunken with the blood of martyrs. This, along with her state of prostitution, helps to identify her. The Bible often describes the worship of false gods as a state of prostitution, and the prophets often leveled this accusation against Israel when they brought in the worship of idols. In general, all nations that have not had the revelation of the true God have worshipped idols. And Satan uses this to his advantage to glean worship for himself and his legions of demons.

Also, Satan has used this condition to aid his fight against God and his attempt to annihilate God's kingdom from the earth. All these ancient empires, which worshipped all kinds of gods, also persecuted the people of the real God. Egypt did it to the Hebrews, as did Assyria and Babylon. Daniel was put into the lions' den over this cause. Rome sacrificed Christians to lions and to fire, and so it has gone.

But the glorious thing is that God strikes back, and he is not only destined to win, but has also been winning for a long time. Revelation 18: 16-18 states,

> *Alas, alas, that great city, that was clothed in fine linen and purple and scarlet, and decked with gold and precious stones and pearls! For in one hour so great riches is come to nought. And every shipmaster, and all the company in ships, and sailors, and as many as trade by sea, stood afar off and cried when they saw the smoke of her burning, saying, what city is like unto this great city!*

Here we have the destruction of idol worship around the world—everywhere the Gospel of Christ has gone. The one hour, as we have seen, refers to the space of time in which the last head on the beast ruled. It was the age of colonial Europe. Everywhere these colonial navies and armies went—Africa, the Americas, India, and the Far East—the old religions fell, and Christianity came in. The process is in no way complete today, of course, but Christianity is the major religion in the world today and, by far, exerts the greatest power and influence through the governments of nations where churches abound.

Chapter 19 of Revelation continues this revelation of mystic, occult religions in the world. Then verse 7 reveals the marriage of the Lamb as being imminent. This will be the consummation of the union of Christ and his church at the time of his return. Resurrection will take place, and those who are alive and in Christ will be carried up with them to meet the Lord in the air, as is declared to us in the resurrection passage, 1 Thessalonians 4:13-18.

Before this occurs, however, John sees heaven opened and Christ descending upon a white horse, equipped for a war—not a wedding. It may be that this passage refers to the going out of the Gospel all through this last age (the one hour). Or it may refer to an explosion of evangelism around the world that is yet to come. The symbol of Christ on the horse combines the symbol of warfare with that of the Word of God, and they have often gone together.

In Revelation 19:19-20 we have this: "And I saw the beast and the kings of the earth and their armies, gathered together to make war against Him that sat upon the horse, and against His army. And the beast was taken, and with him the false prophet that worked miracles before him, with which he deceived those who had the mark of the beast, and those who worshipped his image. These both were cast alive into a lake of fire burning with brimstone."

What war is this? It may have reference to the world wars of the twentieth century. Those wars were clearly a case of the beast against God's people. In both wars, Germany was attempting to remake a Roman-type empire. Hitler horribly persecuted the natural people of God, the Jews. The wars in Korea and Vietnam were against atheistic, anti-God forces. Or the reference may be to a war yet to happen. We will probably soon know the answer to that question. Notice that two of the head demonic powers were cast into the lake of fire. This will happen a thousand years before Satan himself will be going in the lake of fire.

Then we come to chapter 20. At this point, there is nothing unique to add to the volume of material that has been written on this part of Revelation. From the premillennial point of view, chapter 20 marks the time of resurrection of God's saints (the church) and the millennial reign of Christ over the earth. Apparently, the rest of the people of the world will remain, and it will be those people over which Christ and his church will rule. During this wonderful age of extreme good, the world will apparently flourish as it never has before.

Then at the end of that age, the devil, who has been bound during this time, will be released and will gather the nations (not God's people) for a final war against God. That effort will be ended in the same way in which God ended the existence of the city of Sodom.

Then the last judgment takes place, and the dead (not in Christ) are resurrected to stand beside the living (not in Christ) to be finally judged by their works. The result is that they are all cast into the lake of fire while the people of God whose names are in the Book of Life live on to enter a glorious new age that is beyond description.

Chapter 22, which is the last chapter in Revelation, contains some last admonitions to Christians, primary of which is the offer, made yet once again, to come to the water of life, who is the Holy Spirit, and drink of him. The Bible ends with the last recorded heartfelt cry of the Apostle John, as well as all saints of God.

Even so, come, Lord Jesus.